VALUING PEOPLE

VALUING PEOPLE

Citizen Engagement
in Policy Making and Public Service Delivery
in Rural Asia

Michael Anthony Tarallo

authorHOUSE®

AuthorHouse™
1663 Liberty Drive
Bloomington, IN 47403
www.authorhouse.com
Phone: 1-800-839-8640

Published by AuthorHouse 4/13/2012

ISBN: 978-1-4685-5946-0 (e)
ISBN: 978-1-4685-5948-4 (hc)
ISBN: 978-1-4685-5947-7 (sc)

Library of Congress Control Number: 2012904132

Cover photo provided by SeaSkyLab.

This book is printed on acid-free paper.

To my wife, children, and family

for their love and support

In memory of my father

firm believer in

the strength and rights of the underprivileged

michael anthony

tarallo

TABLE OF CONTENTS

ABSTRACT

Citizens do not feel empowered and do not feel they are adequately given the space to meaningfully participate in public governance. Clearly, citizens are not satisfied with the manner in which government is run. This is evident across the developed and developing world, as highlighted also by recent manifestation of discontent in Europe, North America, North Africa, the Middle East, and Asia.

While past government reforms have tendentially focused on performance, efficiency, and productivity, recent developments in public governance have recognized the central role of individuals as '*citizens*' rather than '*customers*' in both the development and implementation of public policies. Although government remains indispensable to governance, citizen can and should play an active role towards solutions to recurring problems as well as emerging and future issues.

A key way to ensure that governments truly reflect the will of the people, particularly the marginalized and the weaker groups of society, is by creating an environment where citizens are given democratic space to exercise '*voice*', even in between elections.

Citizen engagement in decision-making and public service delivery is key to development and to the improvement in the lives of people. The research explicitly selected cases from the largest populated continent in the world, a region where culturally, rights and duties of citizens as well as the power and authority of their political leaders have been significantly influenced by '*Asian values*'. In particular, experiences in citizen engagement in India and Thailand have been respectively further influenced by social stratification (castes) and hierarchical proximity to the monarchy (*sakdhina*). Notwithstanding the extent of democratic values within which the two cases were implemented, both cases are indicative of the potential impact meaningful citizen engagement can have in the lives of ordinary people and carry with them potential for replication.

ABBEVIATIONS AND ACRONYMS

GWIL	Gujarat Water Infrastructure Limited
GWSSB	Gujarat Water Supply and Sewerage Board
ISA	Implementing Support Agency
IWUG	Integrated Water User Group
JMC	Joint Management Committee for Irrigation
LAO	Local Administrative Organization
NBS	National Broadcasting Services
NGO	Non-governmental organizations
NPM	New Public Management
OECD	Organisation for Cooperation and Development
PIM	Participatory Irrigation Management
PVM	Public Value Management
RID	Royal Irrigation Department
RIO	Regional Irrigation Office
UN	United Nations
VAP	Village Action Plan
VWSC	Village Water and Sanitation Committee
WASMO	Water and Sanitation Management Organisation
WUA	Water User Association
WUG	Water User Group
WUO	Water User Organization

michael anthony

tarallo

Chapter One

Introduction

Citizens in both developed and developing countries have grown dissatisfied over past decades with traditional political participation and the functioning of democracies[1]. 'In northern democracies', as argued by Zipfel and Gaventa[2], 'political participation has been declining steadily. Most people…are disillusioned with the political system and feel they have little or no influence…In parts of the global south…confidence in local government is undermined by political corruption, the gulf between those in power and the lives of ordinary people and the failure to tackle widespread poverty.' As a result 'around the world, there has been an explosion of interest in more participatory forms of governance…[This is primarily due to] 'demands from citizens to have more say in decisions that matter to them [as well as]…the recognition by those in power that community involvement is central to the major challenges of revitalising democracy'[3]. In an effort towards narrowing the gap between values and principles of democracy and realities on the ground, new channels of citizen engagement have emerged in various countries giving rise to new promises for participatory governance. Public governance has made initial steps in response to these demands by moving from public sector reforms that have tendentially focused on performance, efficiency, and productivity, towards recent developments that recognize the value of citizen engagement and the central role of individuals as '*citizens*' rather than '*customers*' in both the development and implementation of public policies. People should not be seen 'only as users or choosers, but as active participants who engage in making and shaping social policy and social provisioning'[4].

By '*citizen engagement*' it is meant '[a]ll measures and/or institutional arrangements that link citizens more directly into the decision-making process of the State as to enable them to influence the public policies and programmes in a manner that impact positively on their economic and social lives'[5].

While societies and political dynamics have changed over time both in size and scope when viewed against the classical democracy of ancient Greece, modern democracy has not yet developed into a fully responsive mechanism to its citizens. Society has, indeed, outgrown what Plato regarded as 'the ideal size of the polis as being 5,040 households' for it being 'divisible by all the numbers between 1 and 10, [thus making] citizens obligations and municipal functions [assignable] to groups of the appropriate scale in…what we would today call governance'[6]. Our understanding of what constitutes '*citizenship*' today has also diverged, to some extent, from Athenian selective and exclusionary model where 'only a small proportion of adult males were citizens, [while] a large segment of adult population (women, foreigners and slaves) did not have political rights'[7].

In more recent times, ordinary citizens' normative right to participate in government affairs stems from Article 1 of the Declaration of the Rights to Development[8] and Article 25 of the International Covenant on Civil and Political Rights[9]. The former states that '[t]he right to development is an inalienable human right by virtue of which every human person and all peoples are entitled to participate in, contribute to and enjoy economic, social, cultural and political development, in which all human rights and fundamental freedoms can be fully realized'. Article 25 more specifically affirms that '[e]very citizen shall have the right and the opportunity…[t]o take part in the conduct of public affairs, directly or through freely chosen representatives'.

The apparent weakness in current representative democracies is that they are not driven by principles that support a government '*of the people*' and '*by the people*'. As argued by Bourgon (2007)[10], '*having a vote* is different from *having a say*' simply because the 'right to vote', inherent with representative-style of government, 'does not imply that people are given a voice on matters that interest them most or that they have a role in the decisions that affect them most directly'. What recourse, then, do citizens have in between elections? As it is perceived today, participation is an ongoing and involving process that will not stand for the passivity dictated by intermediary periods from one election to another.

First termed by Hirschman in 1970, "voice'…refer[s] to the range of measures – such as complaint, organized protest, lobbying, and participation in decision-making and product delivery – used by civil society actors to put pressure on service providers to demand better service outcomes'[11]. Giving '*voice*' to citizens, particularly to the weaker and marginalized groups, means setting a stage whereby 'the engagement with the State moves beyond consultative process to more direct forms of influence over policy and spending decisions, service delivery, the monitoring of programme impacts, and accounting for public expenditures'[12].

Citizen engagement in public governance promises an 'enrich[ment of] the practice of representative democracy...[as] it broadens the base of support and reduces the political risks associated to ambitious new initiatives'[13]. While government remains central to society, citizens no longer perceive themselves as passive clients or consumers of government services but rather as an active force towards solutions to handle emerging issues more effectively. Recognizing that '[n]o government can claim to have all the tools, nor all the powers necessary to affect complex and effective policy outcomes', especially in a modern global society, Bourgon (2008)[14] perceives citizens as '*agents of change*' necessary to tackle issues that 'require a change of societal behavior...[or] when the nature and scale of issues exceeds the legislative authority of the state and the government's ability to act...[*e.g.*] global warming and poverty alleviation,...prevention of obesity, wellness and labour productivity,...'safe streets', civic participation and community development'. To this end, greater and meaningful engagement by citizens in public governance requires innovative institutional mechanisms, processes and policies.

The book aims to address the following questions – (i) What major factors account for greater citizen engagement in policy making and public service delivery? (ii) In what ways does citizen engagement in public governance matter?

Principles and strategies of citizen engagement in public governance will be addressed in this research by analyzing not only challenges of governance and public administration systems in general, but also by examining a number of innovative practices in rural Asia, with a particular focus on citizen participation in policy development and implementation in the water sector.

The largest and the most populous continent in the world, Asia comprises culturally and religiously diverse countries that range economically from great wealth to extreme poverty, and politically from the oldest non-Western democracies to oppressive regimes[15]. What is interesting about Asia in general is that '[e]conomically...a number of countries...achieved unprecedented growth and social modernization under authoritarian rule' as compared to 'their peers in other regions'[16]. Culturally, the '*Asian values*' of 'family and community over individuals, discipline and hierarchy over freedom and equality, and consensus and harmony over diversity and conflict' 'have historically played a significant role in prioritizing and justifying the rights and duties of individual citizens and the power and authority of their political leaders'[17]. Against this backdrop, citizen participation and democratization assumes a different connotation in Asia, where democracy is 'equated...with benevolent or soft authoritarian rule'[18]. Notwithstanding, Asia remains the region that is more often recognized in the United Nations' ambit for its innovative practices in public administration, including citizen participation in governance. In fact, over a period spanning nine years since 2003, Asia alone provided 35 examples out of 98 from developing countries duly recognized by the United Nations (UN) for the region's commitment, both at state and citizenry level, towards innovative practices in public administration and governance[19]. For this reason, it is worth reviewing why and how Asia stands out within a realm that is not necessarily Asia's more renowned strength – democratization.

The research focuses on the water sector in Asia's rural areas, with particular emphasis on potable water and irrigation water management. This is so because 'two million people die from waterborne diseases and billions more suffer illnesses – most are children under five'[20]. With a rural population in Asia of 58 percent[21], efficient and effective water management is of significant concern. Implications are considerable for both India and Thailand as 70 percent[22] and 66 percent[23] of the population live in rural areas, respectively.

With a view to recognize the value that citizens generate when actively involved in shaping and implementing policies, literary review is tailored around two areas – (i) a brief examination of a few major trends that have affected public administration reform and governance; and (ii) the examination of a number of recognized and awarded innovative practices in public governance by citizens in rural India and Thailand. Case analysis is carried out *vis-à-vis* Fung's (2006)[24] 'democracy cube' and issues of democratic governance. The research focuses on India and Thailand as they represent diverse contexts, problems and approaches to democratic governance.

While India is recognized as a consolidated democracy, citizen participation is not fully developed mainly owed to low literacy across the country that hampers qualitative participation[25]. Democracy in Thailand, on the other hand, does not vaunt of a positive democratic standing to start with, stifled both by a cultural view of citizens' role in society which limits their political space and a highly mobilized and controlling aristocracy[26]. Yet, there are several examples whereby initiatives in these countries have been recognized by the United Nations for their excellence in public administration and governance. This recognition potentially makes the contrast between the not-so-enabling environment and citizen participation in governance an interesting topic for review. The case studies form part of a long list of winning and runner up initiatives globally recognized by the

United Nations within the context of the UN Public Service Awards' annual competition.

The research is structured along three main chapters, in addition to the introduction and the conclusion. Chapter Two addresses the first research question by focusing on challenges and trends in citizen engagement in public governance. The analysis captures the (i) modernization of the State, covering the paradigm shift from New Public Management to Public Value Management; and (ii) revitalization of democracy, covering growing demand to make democracy more meaningful and to allow for more opportunities of participation in policy-making decision and service delivery. The main body of the research is captured under Chapters Three and Four. Through case studies, Chapter Three answers the second research question by addressing the value and relevance of citizen engagement through innovative practices in policy making and service delivery in India and Thailand. With due regard to the limited scope of the research, drawing from the case studies, Chapter Four will examine what factors, institutions, and mechanisms make citizen engagement effective in rural Asia.

michael anthony

tarallo

Chapter Two

Citizen engagement in public governance: Challenges and trends

Societal problems are neither few nor simple. Governments are challenged by developments that 'have conspired to cause public sector and civil society innovators to rethink th[e] division between government and citizens, and find ways to thicken the engagement of citizens'[27] in policy making and service delivery. Faced with demands by citizens towards greater involvement in decision-making process as well as the increasing complexities and changes in global environments, the approaches governments consider to address public concerns will inevitably vary from country to country based on 'different philosophies about the role of government in society'[28].

The past several decades 'have been a rich period of experimentation in public administration aimed at making government more efficient, effective, productive, transparent and responsive'[29]. Modern public administration grew from a '*compliance model*' of the early 20th century, to a '*performance model*' of the late 1980s to early 1990s, to a current '*enabling and engaging model*' whereby governments are more frequently called upon to take on board the 'wisdom of the crowds'[30]. The 'growing social gap between citizens on one hand, and politicians, political parties, and governments, on the other' is significant to a point where citizens feel powerless and alienated *vis-à-vis* their representative democratic governments[31]. Citizens want to participate directly in policy decisions that affect their lives and they want to do so *ex ante.*

But what major factors account for greater citizen engagement in policy making and public service delivery? Chapter Two aims to address this question. While others exist, the chapter briefly focuses on two of the leading trends worldwide – (i) the modernization of the state, covering the realignment of public administrations towards a citizen-centered focus, and (ii) the revitalization of democracy in favor of direct citizen participation.

Modernizing the state

Modernizing the state is a challenge. It is a process that aims at marrying efficiency of government structures with effectiveness of results that address emerging societal demands. For quite some time, scholars and governments have debated which public administration approach best addresses public issues. Debates on merits and demerits of New Public Management (NPM) and Public Value Management (PVM) have dominated the last thirty years or so. Contention has flourished around two fundamental concerns – is it a question of whether governments are '*doing things right and cost-effectively*' (primarily the focus of NPM) or whether they are indeed '*doing the right thing*' (a fundamental principle of PVM)?

A controversial characteristic of NPM is that it 'assum[es] the superiority of the private sector and private sector management techniques to those of the public sector and public administration'[32]. Basic principles of NPM can be 'classif[ied]...into three broad categories:

organizational restructuring [*e.g.* downsizing, disaggregation into departments and agencies], the use of market-type mechanisms [*e.g.* privatization, contracting out, user charges], and a focus on performance [*e.g.* performance budgeting and management, outputs, and indicators]'[33].

By contrast, while recognizing merits of private sector's principles rather than its values, PVM does not equate '[g]overning…as the same as shopping or more broadly buying and selling goods in a market economy'[34]. Governing entails more than providing services but rather providing services that matter, where valued social and economic outcomes are advanced[35]. Public value is what the people say it is, and it should therefore be collectively built through citizen engagement.

NPM and PVM have practically little in common. Hood and Peters (2004)[36] argue that NPM has moved into an 'age of paradox'. This is attributed to the fact that actual implementation has come to contradict the very same principles that originally set NPM apart from other public administration philosophies. To begin with, while the replacement of Weberian 'rules-based, process-driven' approach[37] was a central drive for public administration reforms, it has been 'noted that process controls over bureaucracies were in many cases retained and augmented and that increased formality and regulation were imposed on public bureaucracies during the New Public Management[38].

Second, NPM advocates for a 'leaner, and increasingly privatized government, emulating not only the practices but also the values of business'[39]. Pressured by market-oriented competition, according to NPM supporters, small government is achieved through disaggregation

– meaning the act of decentralizing government functions to arms' length agencies (a process known as '*agencification*'). However, under NPM the number of administrative units increased and therefore enlarging the scope of government[40]. Not only has agencification created more complex and dynamic agencies interrelationship, it has also created duplication of expenditures and more bureaucratic leadership positions[41].

On the issue of accountability, for practically the same reason, advocates on either side of the aisle, in a manner of speaking, see it degenerate in the hands of the other. On the one hand, the resulting fragmentation of government under NPM reduces accountability[42]. According to PVM advocates '[a]ccountability comes through more extended [and direct involvement] of citizen' 'and stakeholders in service delivery and decision making'[43]. Supporters of NPM, however, argue that '[g]overnance in the world of public value management is one where no one is in charge but where leaders at various levels play key roles'[44]. Accountability under NPM 'comes through the assessment of management achievement against targets through the measure of performance'[45].

Debate over NPM *vs.* PVM is essentially grouped into three categories – private *vs.* public (including individualism *vs.* plurality), output *vs.* outcomes (including efficiency *vs.* effectiveness), and customer *vs.* citizen (including responsiveness *vs.* collaboration, exclusion *vs.* inclusion, and inequity *vs.* equity).

Private vs. public

By pushing for a minimalist state role, deregulation and privatization, 'NPM takes for granted that measures relevant for and successful in the private sector can be directly transplanted to the public sector without transforming or adapting them'[46]. But, in so doing, NPM blurs the distinction of principles and values between public and private institutions[47]. In many respects it has thoughtlessly done so, for reasons that are more apparent in the discussion regarding both output/outcomes and customer/citizen, below.

'Concepts like individual choice, market, competition, customer sovereignty and exit are very unfitting for the public sector'[48]. Once a major proponent of NPM, even OECD (2003)[49] acknowledged that NPM's influence in promoting 'competitive government models failed to understand that public management arrangements not only deliver public services, but also enshrine deeper governance values'. Achieving public value for the collective is precisely what sets the public sector apart from the private one, whose goal is to achieve economic advantage for the benefit of the individual.

Output vs. outcomes

In debating NPM and PVM, particular emphasis is placed on their respective view on output and outcomes. Outcomes 'encompass much higher order aspirations (*e.g.* national security, poverty reduction, or public health)' than output[50]. For instance, while the private sector focuses on efficient and effective ways to collect garbage (output), the public sector's primary concern is to safeguard public health (outcome)[51].

The production of output is directly linked to efficiency. While PVM 'does not have the immediate sharpness about how to meet efficiency demands'[52], 'extensive literature on privatization, contracting, and the use of markets [under NPM] lacks evidence of any real efficiency gains'[53]. While no one 'wants a wasteful and inefficient state,...NPM doctrines...fail to recognize that efficiency is a relative concept that is based on the concept of appropriateness' – in other words, it can be called 'efficiency' if certain *outcomes for society at large are achieved with minimum of resources*[54].

Under PVM, therefore, public managers, 'in searching for public value...are asking more than whether procedures have been followed [which denotes a focus on *input*, typical of traditional public administration]. They are asking more than whether their targets have been met [which denotes a focus on *output*, typical of NPM]. They are asking[, instead, whether] their actions are bringing a net benefit to society [which denotes a focus on *outcomes*, typical of PVM]'[55].

Customer vs. citizen

Classifying citizens as '*customers*' creates complications. The concept 'implies the priority of individual choices over collective citizenship rights, excludes the entitlement of disadvantage groups, and depoliticizes people by stressing individualistic preferences'[56].

'The term...*customer*,...contradicts the very basic notion of belonging, altruism, contribution to society, and self-derived participation in citizenry actions. When someone is identified as a [customer], he or she is not actively engaged in social initiatives, but is merely a passive service (or product) consumer, dependent on the goodwill and interest of the owner'[57]. By contrast, Pollitt (1995)[58] argues that 'since the NPM principle of "customer responsiveness"...requires that the degree of user satisfaction with public services be measured,' 'citizens [do, in fact, directly] participate in the process of evaluating public services…[i]f the results of user evaluation feed back to the policy-making process.' What Pollitt's argument fails to capture, however, is that citizen participation, to be meaningful to decision-making, should be *ex ante* rather than *ex post facto.*

Furthermore, 'the relationship between government and its citizens is not the same as that between a business and its customers'[59]. Contrary to the private sector, '[i]n the public sector, it is problematic to even determine who the customer is, because government serves more than just the immediate client. Government also serves those who may be waiting for service, those who may need the service even though they are not actively seeking it, future generations of service recipients, relatives and friends of the immediate recipient, and on and on.'

When viewed *vis-à-vis* '*equality*' and '*inclusion*', Argyriades (2003)[60] argues that the market 'paradigm does little to highlight' 'two of the cardinal values of democratic governance'. While 'competition can help achieve parsimony in resource use…, improve the quality of public services,…[as well as] allow…citizens (as customers or users) more scope to "exit" from one provider to another'[61], 'not all citizens can qualify as customer or clients as there are low-income families whose income have not improved'[62]. As services are driven by 'the socioeconomic status of customers'[63], in the absence of 'political change,…the poor and the politically weak…will continue to be poorly served'[64]. While a 'democratic State is clearly not at liberty to favour or discriminate'[65] public consumerism under NPM does little to reduce the gap between those who can afford services and those who cannot.

Lastly, Fountain (2001)[66] argues that while '[c]ustomer models attend to immediate gratification of consumer tastes' and 'customers have no obligation, legal or moral, to understand, to build, or to participate in the institutions that provide goods and services', the roles of citizens is quite the opposite. In fact, citizens not only have the right and obligation, through participation, to 'safeguard…their public institutions' but also the 'obligat[ion] to make choices on behalf of, or representing, future [citizens]'.

'The challenge', argues Fountain (2001)[67], 'is to increase efficiency and responsiveness in ways that strengthen democracy, rather than weakening it'. NPM has tendentially brought about a weakened democracy for having undervalued the role of individuals as '*citizens*'. This weakness has pushed ordinary people to get involved and be vocal about their concerns, calling for an active participation in decision-making and service delivery for what is of value to them and future generations rather than what is perceived to be by their governments and their elected representatives.

Revitalizing democracy

Debate over the various forms of democracy has generally revolved around the dichotomy between representative and direct democracy[68]. While the former emphasizes governance through elected representation, the latter 'argues that citizens themselves can make wise decisions on political matters, whether through referenda, town meetings, citizen initiatives, or other direct means'[69].

The concept of democracy has evolved over the last two and a half millennia since its birth in the fifth century B.C. in Greece. Democracy in Greek city-states was based on direct participation in decision-making by its citizens in popular assemblies but was limited to a small number of the male adult population. By contrast, modern democracies, developed in nation-states with large geographical areas and large populations, make citizens' direct participation in decision-making problematic, thus favoring representation instead. Modern democracy differs from the classical model at least on two counts – representation and complexity. Representation in modern democracy is based on a more inclusive definition of citizenship that captures all adult males and, in recent times, females as well. The magnitude and complexities of socio-economic character of modern decision-making also set modern democracy apart from classical Greek democracy[70].

'What distinguishes democracy from other political regimes', as argued by May (1978)[71], 'is its creation of a necessary correspondence between acts of governance and the equally weighted felt interests of citizens with regard to these acts' guaranteed by the 'institutional mechanism…[of] the democratic election'. Through this mechanism, the electors have '[t]he power to select representatives and punish them retrospectively' thus giving them 'a certain influence in enforcing their interests'. In the process, 'political responsibility and decision-making has been delegated to rather narrow groups or even individuals occupying strategic positions within the state'[72]. This is particularly owed to the fact that, as it is argued, a special kind of 'expertise is required to understand policy options or policy content even in the most general terms...[and] citizens are neither capable nor prepared to commit their time and personal resources to participation in the very complex analysis and decision-making process'[73].

The downfall of the concept of representative democracy is that it has weakened the founding principles of democracy – *i.e.* government '*of the people*' and '*by the people*'[74]. In fact, '[i]n between elections,... representatives are free to vote in the public policies they and not electors want'[75]. This phenomenon can be captured by what Merton (1940)[76] termed 'goal displacement'. The latter occurs when the operational focus on the *means* (in this case, representative democracy) displaces the organizational strategic focus on the *ends* (popular welfare and will enshrined in the founding principles of democracy), which the means were originally supposed to support.

Representative democracy brought about signs of distress and distrust in government on the part of citizenries around the world, which is evidenced by the decreasing participation in political parties and turnout in election voting, known as 'democratic deficit'[77] or 'aversion for politics'[78]. This malaise is rooted in a number of factors. Fundamentally, the disengagement in political life is driven by citizens' feeling of disempowerment *vis-à-vis* and dissatisfaction with representative democratic system. This is so because 'institutions fail to provide meaningful avenues of participation and genuine involvement in public life'[79], and representatives 'do not react at all, or react in an unsatisfactory way to existing issues'[80] causing citizens to lose trust in their elected representatives.

Since the 1960s, citizens have been calling for a return to a direct participation in decision-making process, which had been stifled for the most part with the surge of representative democracy in the eighteenth century. While 'return' to classical democracy is an oversimplification, the current phase of democracy does stem from the original principle of direct participation but on a much broader scale and scope than that practiced in ancient Greece.

What many citizens in both developed and developing world want is a better government by popular demand where decisions on every-day issues that affect them take into account and are influenced by their own preferences rather than those perceived by government officials. The demand is reflected in the actions taken by citizens towards change. Citizens' proposition for change is an iterative process *en face* shortfalls in the way government does business. At the foundation of this process is awareness – of rights, of information – which can change the dynamics of power. Poor people, as in the case of Bangladesh, have grown 'a different understanding of things…[and] the rich cannot put pressure on the poor in the way that they used to'[81]. New awareness and skills lead to new forms of action as in the case of anti-apartheid citizens movements in South Africa which were able to secure new rights and 'public recognition of HIV/AIDS as a health issue' as well as securing 'access to publicly-supplied anti-retroviral medicines to 60,000 people'[82]. Being vocal and active may lead to solidarity across countries as in the case of the Global Campaign for Education[83] and 'peasant associations…who have allowed farmers to challenge the World Bank on several controversial issues'[84]. In the struggle for land reform in the Philippines, 'peasant organizations and NGOs [were] able to initiate a dialogue with the government agency…[and] to form a working committee to implement new reforms' which led 'to access to land and livelihoods for poor farmers'[85]. Citizen mobilization and engagement contributed in many cases to national policy change leading to access to public goods and housing in Brazil[86], as well as budget reforms on maternal mortality at the national level in Mexico[87]. In the developed world, as well, response by citizens to government inadequacies has led the successful mobilization of residents in the United Kingdom to maintain access to health services by keeping a health centre open[88] and 'the passage of the 'living-wage' ordinances, leading to increased incomes for the working poor' in the United States[89]. These are only but a few examples of how citizen demands for change have actually contributed to reforms in policy and service delivery.

With 'a growing demand [by] citizens to be involved in decision-making processes which affect their lives', there has been a 'rapid and far-reaching' spread of consultative mechanisms in the form of 'community health councils, parent committees in schools, tenant councils, and countless other beneficiary committees'[90]. Since the initial movement of the 1960s and 1970s, 'the concept of participation [has increasingly begun] to move from one of users and choosers of service provided by others, to one in which people became actors and agents in broader processes of governance'[91]. Through actively taking part in democracy, citizens can directly select policies which best reflect their needs and satisfy their demands for greater transparency, responsiveness, and accountability in public institutions governance.

Citizen participation has been globally recognized 'as an important governance norm that can strengthen the decision-making arrangements of the state and produce outcomes that favour the poor and the disadvantaged'[92]. What is important is that participation does not limit itself simply to voting[93] nor should we be fooled into thinking that the mere presence of elections renders countries as full democracies[94]. Participation instead is a process that requires an active engagement of the citizenry in an 'open dialogue...[where] individuals have a voice in the decisions that affect them'[95]. Barber (1984)[96], however, argues that while participation is essential in governance, its weight does not necessarily require that citizens take part directly 'at every level and in every instance, but frequently enough and in particular when basic policies are being decided and when significant power is being deployed'.

Barber (1984)[97] argues that participation of citizens in governance is important for three basic reasons. First, by actively engaging in the fashioning of laws and policies, both laws and policies become 'democratically valuable. When they secure the active agreement of citizens, laws yield superior outcomes from the perspective of each party.' It follows then that the solutions to issues also become 'valuable because the parties created [them] themselves.' Lastly, Barber argues that engagement fosters transformation within each party about the other. The act of deliberating, for instances, creates opportunities for 'each party to gain...an appreciation for the needs...desires and dispositions' of others resulting in a re-appreciation of their own values and their reorganization towards the potential 'creation of common goals, public ends, and provisional, flexible consensus'.

'While democracy is not the only means by which improved governance can be achieved, it is the only viable one'[98]. To this end, Adam (1997)[99], argues that '[g]overnments which solicit the public input in policy-making processes, are eventually able to accomplish more by virtue of public participation'. This is so based on a four-pronged approach that addresses the (i) development of national development goals, (ii) provision of appropriate mechanisms and channels for governmental succession, (iii) establishment of political legitimacy, and (iv) accountability[100]. While the first approach brings about broader societal aspirations and priorities, appropriate mechanisms and channels 'provide incentives to protect the capacity, reliability and integrity of core state institutions, including civil service, the legal system and the democratic process itself.' Similarly, through political legitimacy, 'democracy strengthens [governments'] capacity to carry out their policies and functions efficiently and effectively.' Lastly, when governments are 'accountable to citizens, democracy makes them more responsive to popular concerns and provides added incentives for transparency in decision-making'.

When compared, experiences in democracy and freedoms for citizen participation in India and Thailand vary. Overall, for instance, India is recognized 'as a stable and consolidated democracy', classified as one of the 89 'fully free' countries according to a 2009 Freedom House survey[101]. It is a country where 'more than a majority of its citizens feel they enjoy equal rights, freedom of speaking out their minds and the political right of choosing the government they like... [and approves] the way Indian democracy works'[102]. Nevertheless, Bhattacharyya (2006)[103] argues that, while democracy in India may be consolidated, citizen participation is not fully developed and it is hampered by low literacy across the country, which makes it difficult for 'the development of the rationality that is required for qualitative participation'. Democracy in Thailand, on the other hand, is recognized as weak particularly since the more recent *coup d'etats* in 2006. Even more striking is the country's unique '*sakdhina*' highly structured class system – related to the proximity to the monarchy – whereby citizens' role in society, as a key to good society, is to 'know their place'[104]. By definition 'Thais are by no means born to citizenship as equals' and have a limited political space by design. As argued by Albritton and Bureekul (2008)[105], the political arena is culturally regarded as 'immoral in nature as it represents an arena of contention and conflict of interests...[and] by reducing the space of political participation,...[the] government is left to the appropriate instruments of the monarchy – the military and the bureaucracy.' As a result, the participation of citizens in Thailand is culturally stifled and 'difficult to sustain [particularly when also] confronted with a highly mobilized aristocracy controlling the instruments of force'[106].

Concluding remarks

As noted above, the 'managerialism' of the New Public Management 'has widened the distance between government and citizens'[107] as well as the 'gap between public expectation and perceived governmental performance...[This gap has generally contributed] to the decline of public trust' in government[108]. Despite being a heavily criticized paradigm, NPM's principles of efficiency, effectiveness, and economizing remain important and essential. It is running governments like a business that suffered criticisms in favor of a more inclusive and equitable style – the Public Value Management paradigm. This latter paradigm resonates with the surge in the demand by citizens for greater *ex ante* participation in decision-making process.

Taking into account the fact that governments do not have all the capacity, resources and reach to govern all on their own, engaging citizens in the decision-making process and public service delivery could be the only viable option. Governments should recognize this. As argued by Bourgon (2007)[109], governments play a key role in encouraging citizen engagement. On the one hand, governments need to create an enabling environment by regarding citizens as 'more than constituents, voters or clients...[by] remov[ing] obstacles to the participation of groups most frequently excluded: the youth,...the poor,...[and] those affected by special barriers due to age, handicaps, distance, literacy', among others. On the other hand, governments must establish clear 'rules of engagement [to] help clarify how the commitment to citizen engagement is given shape in practice in the decision-making process of an organization'[110].

Within the context of democratic experimentation in India and Thailand, as briefly noted above, Chapter Three addresses how citizen participation in these countries has made a difference. This review should provide an interesting outlook on citizen involvement in decision-making and service delivery *en face* highlighted constraints. The following chapter covers innovative practices which have been recognized and awarded at the global level by the United Nations as shining exemplars of citizen engagement practices.

Chapter Three

Valuing citizen engagement in policy making and public service delivery

Redford (1969)[111] argues that public participation in a democratic society supports what he calls 'democratic morality'. Democratic morality, he contends, is based on three basic premises. First, it 'assumes that the individual is the basic measure of human value…[; second,] that all persons have full claim to the attention of the system [regardless of their wealth and social status; and third] that individual claims can best be promoted through the involvement of all persons in the decision-making process'. This argument is embodied by Public Value Management which regards 'citizen engagement…as an appropriate and necessary part of policy [design and] implementation in a democracy'[112] and essential for 'the creation and maintenance of a self-governing political community'[113].

The question, however, remains – 'Why is there really value in engaging citizens in democratic governance?' Citizen engagement can be valued as having both an *intrinsic* and an *instrumental* value. According to Osmani (2008)[114] '[t]he intrinsic value refers to the idea that the act of participation is valuable in itself', meaning 'it is the right thing to do according to democratic ideals' as it builds both citizenship and community[115]. As argued by Lucio (2009)[116], participation provides 'a vehicle to help individual community members become "citizens"', in other words, assuming 'a way of thinking and acting that is characterized by openness to opposing ideas, collaboration, and a sense of responsibility to others'[117]. The second value attributed to citizen engagement is that of being *instrumental*. Within the context of '*governance*', it is recognized that governments are not in a position to solve public problems alone. That said, participation becomes instrumental in gaining support, cooperation, and legitimacy of public initiatives, policy approval and implementation[118]. As argued by Osmani (2008)[119], 'one of the pitfalls of top-down bureaucratic decision-making', [is that 'd]ecisions based on wrong perceptions of what people actually want can result in wastage of scarce resources... When people are able to exercise their voice in the conduct of public affairs, they will have an opportunity to reveal their true preferences. Only participation can allow this exercise of voice'. Goetz and Gaventa (2001)[120], however, argue that 'citizen initiatives to improve public sector accountability and responsiveness are never independent of the state...[T]he range of action open to citizens, and even the forms of associational life citizen choose, are shaped by the nature of the political regime, the variation in the enjoyment of citizenship rights between categories of citizen, and the institutional capacity of the bureaucracy to make any kind of response at all.' This is evident in the cases below.

Within this context, Chapter Three addresses the second research question – '*In what ways does citizen engagement in public governance matter?*' To this end, two cases are presented to highlight ways in which citizen engagement has made a difference in both decision-making and public service delivery in rural India and Thailand. While the cases offer only but a glimpse on the potential of citizen engagement, they do provide insight into the kind of efforts ordinary citizens make to place their participation on the governance map, to enhance their footprint, and to meaningfully support the public interest. The cases were selected from a long list of initiatives recognized by the United Nations Public Service Award programme for their contribution towards fostering participation in policy decision-making by implementing new processes and institutional mechanisms that channel demands and views of its citizens.

Citizen engagement in India

Gaining independence in 1950, democracy in India began 'with a great promise to secure to all its citizens social, economic and political justice, liberty of thought, expression, belief and worship, and equality of status and opportunity'[121]. The constitution provides for all of its citizens the guarantees of fundamental rights and 'outlaws the traditional system of social stratification based on caste, and prohibits discrimination on the grounds of religion, language, race, ethnic background, gender or place of birth'[122]. That said, however, India remains the largest democracy in the world with structurally embedded socioeconomic inequalities[123] based on over 3,000 castes and sub-castes as well as over 600 tribes[124].

Although results of a 2005 survey would argue that the majority of sampled citizens are satisfied with democracy in India, it is also true that 'nearly one-third of the respondents do not think…everyone in the country enjoys equal rights or [is] free to speak out…views and opinions'[125]. The same survey indicates that almost sixty percent of the respondents feel that most people do not avail of basic necessities in life[126]. Sadashiva (2010)[127] argues that owing to the caste structure, India still faces 'deeply entrenched inequality in power relations, as well as the oppressive and exploitative forms of production and feudalization'. With a literacy rate of just over 50 percent[128], women are among those who suffer the most as they are accorded 'subordinate and discriminatory status…in Indian society, in terms of social relations, political positions and economic activities'[129].

While citizen engagement, particularly in rural India, is addressed by the 73rd Constitutional Amendment Act of 1992 for the first time on a national scale[130], active participation in policy making has been both challenging and minimal[131]. Bhattacharyya (2006)[132] argues that this is mainly owed to low literacy, which has contributed to the poor quality of participation and poor level of social harmony, exacerbated by 'primordial loyalties to language, religion, caste, and ethnic groups'. The Act was part of the government's decentralization efforts 'to establish a real participatory democracy by transferring the decision-making powers…to the people' down to the village level[133]. The Act also ensures 'a quota for representation of women and persons of scheduled castes and tribes in local governments of 33 percent apiece'[134].

A second major effort on the part of the government to create conditions for participation in India was the enactment of the Right to Information Act of 2005 which regards access to public information as a 'critical prerequisite in achieving the ideals of participatory democracy, since without adequate and accurate information, citizens are neither able to exercise their rights nor participate meaningfully and effectively in public decision-making process affecting their lives'[135]. Ironically, only 3 percent of the rural population, which constitute 70 percent[136] of the entire population, and 33 percent of the urban population were even aware of the Act in 2009[137].

Within this context, notwithstanding, the following case highlights a positive outcome of India's efforts to enable a more meaningful citizen engagement down to the level of the village.

Case 1 - Institutionalization of community managed drinking water supply and user level water quality monitoring

The '*Institutionalization of community managed drinking water supply and user level water quality monitoring*' initiative in Gujarat State, India, by the Water and Sanitation Management Organisation (WASMO) received recognition both at the national[138] and international levels[139]. Devised by the government to meet challenges posed by drought and water scarcity, the initiative is recognized as a 'sound partnership between the State and the people…where power, resources and responsibilities [related to rural drinking water quality, access, and availability] have been transferred to the community'[140].

The initiative was adopted to address poor rural drinking water supply systems, which up to 2002, when WASMO was established, failed to provide clean water accessibility and availability in rural areas. Exacerbated by a twenty-six-year drought period over the last seventy-five years, problems with water issues in Gujarat cover salination ingress, contamination by high levels of fluoride and nitrite, over-drafting of ground water for agriculture, and depletion of aquifers[141], leading to a water crisis marked by competition and conflict[142].

With a heavy dependency on ground water (constituting 78 percent of water supply in rural Gujarat, of which only 2 percent is used as potable water), issues of quality and access are of major concern, especially when about 80 percent of common diseases are water-borne[143]. Compounding these issues are institutional capacity and operational deficiencies, as well as a lack of involvement on the part of the communities[144].

From an institutional perspective, '[p]ublic health engineering departments and state water boards, which had been driving the centralist approach to water supply since independence, were considered monopolistic, overstaffed and lacking accountability to users, especially the poor, marginalized groups and women'[145]. Prior to the current initiative, while the government was responsible for creating and maintaining water supply systems, lack of manpower[146] and vast distances made delivery and maintenance challenging and ineffective[147]. Services were irregular and unable to meet the requirements of the communities[148]. Furthermore, results of water surveillance activities were not shared with the user community[149]. From the community perspective, on the other hand, the government's rigid bureaucratic structure has resulted in a strong sense of complacency[150], lack of trust in the government[151], and a total lack of participation on the part of the user communities[152]. Lack of participation has also resulted in lack of awareness and issues of exclusion, equity, and gender[153]. Furthermore, 'the indiscriminate exploitation of water for irrigation…and the increasing identification of the state as water provider…led to the alienation of communities from the management of their water resources'[154].

Faced with all these challenges and under-achievements, the first step for change came from the government. Accepting its limitations, the government recognized that 'community managed rural water supply could not be [by definition] a one-man show of the [g]overnment [but rather]…it would require a partnership…[with] the community…

and regional NGOs'[155] where, most importantly, communities' views and wisdom are included in the development programme[156]. Within this context, the government instituted WASMO to actively 'promote new mind-sets capable of a genuine paradigm shift in the [water] sector' from provider to facilitator[157]. The shift was also reflected in the expertise of its staff – from a technical one dominated by engineers to a 'special emphasis...given to the social sciences to address the need for social mobilization and constructive dialogue with the community [in the fields of environmental planning and management]'[158]. WASMO heavily relies on capacity building programmes for both its organizational staff as well as the user communities[159]. Decentralization and devolution of funds were key factors in the success of this initiative. Decision-making power was transferred to the villages (*panchayat*) for all matters concerning water supply and sanitation, including water quality testing and monitoring[160]. Funds were transferred directly to the villages, consciously bypassing the district level (*takula panchayat*), the second layer of the local administration[161].

The initiative involves a number of stakeholders. The entire rural community of Gujarat, particularly women, children, and lower caste families, are the primary stakeholders. Women and girls are particularly affected by water shortage issue as they are the family members responsible for fetching water, often for long distances, for household requirements. This uneasy access to water places additional strain on women and girls related to domestic responsibilities and school attendance. Lower caste families are also affected because they are usually excluded from development initiatives. The government is represented by WASMO, the Gujarat Water Supply and Sewerage Board (GWSSB), and Gujarat Water Infrastructure Limited (GWIL).

The third set of stakeholder comprises the NGO community specialized in drinking water and water resource management, who act as Implementing Support Agencies (ISAs)[162].

Gram panchayat (village assembly) approves the Village Action Plan (VAP) based on Participatory Rural Appraisals which provide the community the opportunity to 'identify...needs and problems,... analyse the situation, bring conflict to the fore, understand each other's perspectives and also resolve issues through an open dialogue at the very onset of the programme'[163]. *Pani samitis* – which are water committees and mandatorily include women and marginalized groups under the 73rd Constitutional Amendment[164] – are responsible for the implementation, including monitoring and supervising structural works, procuring materials, preparing contracting schedules, as well as managing funds and maintain all accounting records[165]. WASMO facilitates village initiatives, provides 90 percent of capital investment in addition to the community's 10 percent contribution, and is responsible for the technical clearance of water structures. The GWSSB and GWIL are responsible for the bulk transfer of water up to the village level[166]. NGOs are involved in providing support in issues related to social mobilization, communication, capacity development, participatory rural appraisals, assisting in developing VAPs, and technical support[167].

Comprehensive participation in decision-making processes is ensured through *gram sabhas* (village meetings) where the community has an opportunity to exercise voice, reflect on their needs, resolve conflicts, and carry social audits of the *pani samitis*[168]. Through the *gram sabhas* '[e]very important decision taken by the *pani samiti* is vetted and approved...so as to ensure equity and transparency and a wider acceptance of the programme' and it occurs on six different occasions. These involve the 'acceptance of the programme; formation of the *pani samitis*; information sharing on works to be taken up, decisions on estimated expenditures and community participation; approval of the VAP; commissioning of scheme and sharing of final accounts, and decisions related to [operations and management] and water tariff'[169]. Particularly on water tariffs, the community has the discretion to apply differential rates to cater for disadvantaged groups that do not have the capacity to pay[170]. Furthermore, the mandatory 10 percent contribution towards capital costs in village projects 'ensure[s] that the communities not only own the structures, but also participate in the project from the very beginning'. This has a two-fold effect. First, as the community is required 'to deposit... contribution[s] before construction commences, the community will ensure that only those structures are created for which they have a need...[Second, as] the community bears the cost, every person can question implementation, as well as check accounts and procedures at any point in time'[171].

The project was able to produce significant outputs and outcomes. In six years up to 2009, a total of 13,542 (or 75 percent) community institutions in the form of Village Water and Sanitation Committees (VWSCs) were established against a total of 18,000 villages state-wide. This was coupled with strong partnerships with about 75 non-governmental organizations and the State[172]. So what difference did these outputs actually make in the lives of people? A clear and enabling paradigm shift in the government's role as facilitator rather than provider, whereby powers, resources and responsibilities have been transferred to the community, produced a number of benefits to the community. Independent evaluations revealed that about 50 percent of the population is now covered with household level tap water connectivity[173]; all villages have 24-hours water availability within the village, sparing women from walking long distance to fetch water, on average about 5-6 kilometers[174]; issues of sanitation and hygiene at household level and behavior of school children markedly improved[175]; water-borne diseases were eliminated; poverty alleviated; transparent governance was enhanced; child mortality and morbidity were reduced; villagers have more time for their work and income levels increased; there has been a reduction in time girls spend helping their mothers in fetching water, coupled with an increase in their enrolment and attendance in schools to nearly 100 percent[176].

Citizen engagement in Thailand

With elections in 2007, a 'semblance of democracy was restored' in Thailand one year after the military took over in a coup. With 60 percent support received and rejection from the largest rural area in Thailand's northeastern region, the newly adopted constitution was essentially drafted by a junta-appointed committee[177]. The qualitative prospect of Thailand's democratic wave is conditioned by both historical and cultural factors. '[S]cholars…underline the non-existence in the Thai setting of what can be called 'civil society' in 'Western' terms, at least up to the end of the 1980s'[178] when, 'with the demise of the Thai Communist Party,...the country experienced a relaxation towards civil society movements'[179]. Since the 1980s, 'a process of decentralization has been put in place in the attempt to curb the power of the bureaucracy and promote local autonomy'[180]. Nonetheless, Connors[181] argues that decentralization in Thailand is simply another form of 'democrasubjection', meaning 'the subjection of people to imaginary forms of self-rule' where 'a top-down approach [is] depicted as a bottom-up process'[182]. '[G]enuine grassroots participation in the decision-making process', in fact, is curbed by powerful politicians, bureaucrats and rich people[183].

Essentially, Thai culture is 'based on fundamental inequalities, not explicitly on wealth, but on status derived from proximity to the monarchy' captured by the '*sakdhina*' hierarchical system as a function of 'place' or status whereby 'everyone knows to pay proper respect to 'superiors'' and accepts and is content with 'the status to which they are born'[184]. The 'king is the moral compass of the nations...[As such] there is no need for democratic political structures.' It follows that the principle governing both 'government' and 'administration' is that, while 'democratically...elected governments come and go,... bureaucracy is the one constant in Thai polity'[185]. The implication, therefore, is that '[g]uardians of the '*sakdhina*' system [meaning, the aristocracy comprised of monarchy, bureaucracy and the military] work assiduously to ensure that government in Thailand is weak' since 'strong government threatens the autonomy of the bulwarks of the aristocracy'[186]. That said, the masses present a threat. Conversely, however, even if the masses were to organize, '[p]opular democracy... [would be] difficult to sustain when confronted by a highly mobilized aristocracy controlling the instruments of force'[187]. As a result, citizen engagement in decision-making is hindered, if not suffocated, by public institutions and power structures that heavily rely on Thai's patron-client social relations[188].

Within this context, the following case is significant because it runs counter to current Thai's 'democratic moralism'. Furthermore, established in 2004, the initiative not only continues to exemplify authentic participatory governance down to the individual level, it also runs counter to earlier failed attempts in participatory irrigation management that were implemented in more democratic times in Thailand.

Case 2: Participatory irrigation management

As in the case in India, the '*Participatory Irrigation Management*' (PIM) initiative in the Suphan Buri Province, Thailand, received recognition both at the national[189] and international levels[190]. Borne from a government initiative, PIM is an irrigation water management system that encourages efficient allocation and effective use of water in the agricultural sector by integrating 'the participation of water users at all phases of irrigation management such as planning, operation, maintenance, monitoring and evaluation'[191].

The initiative was adopted to address the poor and inequitable irrigation water management which failed to immediately respond to farmers' needs[192]. There are a number of factors that contributed to this failure. First, irrigation water management up to 2004 was under the exclusive and non-participatory authority of the Royal Irrigation Department (RID)[193]. The Department's Regional Irrigation Offices (RIO) held complete decision-making power, did not encourage public participation at any phase, disregarded existing traditional water user organizations[194], and dictated the establishment of new ones[195]. In essence, RIO officials being in 'a position of superiority over the less-educated local people'[196], were simply uncooperative[197]. Furthermore, RIO 'was unable to provide irrigated water in a sufficient and timely manner[198] for being understaffed[199] and for lacking technical skills in planning, implementing, and monitoring as well as poor people-management skills[200]. Second, perceiving irrigation water management as a state-initiated and state-oriented scheme, farmers had no sense of ownership, had no access to information, and did not maintain and, in fact, destroyed irrigation structures[201]. Owing to the lack of adequate water, tension increased when 'individual farmers strived to get water for their own plots without caring for the needs of fellow farmers'[202].

The strength in this latest PIM initiative as compared to earlier versions in Thailand is that it shifts its quantitative focus of building new irrigation projects to qualitative approaches towards the effective use of irrigation water based on active citizen engagement, capacity development, and appropriate technology[203]. This is achieved through the active involvement of farmers in water management decision-making at every phase and level of the irrigation water system[204]. Under this new scheme, RIO maintains a technical advisory role while farmers, through the Joint Management Committee for Irrigation (JMC), have a primary opportunity to exercise voice[205].

The initiative is implemented by four key stakeholders – the Royal Irrigation Department (RID, through RIO), water user organizations (WUOs, which include water user groups/WUGs and integrated water user groups/IWUGs), JMC, and local administrative organizations (LAOs). The water irrigation management is planned, organized, maintained, monitored, and evaluated by 1 JMC, 9 IWUGs, 278 WUGs, and 6,640 members[206].

Responsibilities are set across three levels, *i.e.* reservoir, canal, and ditch[207]. At the reservoir level, the key players are JMC and RIO. JMC, which comprises representatives of IWUGs, RIO, LAOs, and relevant public and private agencies, has the final say in allocating irrigation water in each crop season, scheduling water distribution, disseminating information, determining control measures for water use at the reservoir level, as well as considering the irrigation system's modernization and maintenance needs. RIO, on the other hand, carries out technical advisory functions as well as being responsible for procuring water supply, and operation and maintenance[208]. At the canal level, IWUGs and RIO manage water at the primary, secondary, or tertiary canals. IWUGs are responsible for the coordination among irrigation users, RIO, LAOs, and other public agencies as well as ensuring an equitable distribution of water allocation. RIO, in particular, acts as the regulator at a primary canal and is responsible for constructing and maintaining canals, drainage channels, and irrigation structures, as well as supervising water distribution. At the ditch level, WUGs are the sole entity responsible for ditch management and maintenance[209]. At the provincial, district, and municipal levels, LAOs are responsible for allocating funds for the maintenance of irrigation infrastructures.

Opportunities for participatory water irrigation planning, organization, maintenance, monitoring, and evaluation occur at three determinate periods in a crop season – before, during, and after[210]. *Before* each major crop season, WUGs – each of which can comprise five to more than 30,000 farmers in a water user association (WUA)[211], – are notified of the initial draft plan for water allocation by RIO based on the amount of water in the reservoir. WUGs compile allocation and maintenance proposals and submit to IWUGs. The latter make a plan for each canal and, together with RIO they adjust the plan to respond to the needs of WUGs. Lastly, JMC approves the plan on water allocation, sets the rules for obtaining irrigation water and then distributes to relevant parties water allocation agreements, rules, and maintenance notices. *During* each major crop season, WUGs routinely monitor members' individual water consumption, receive confirmation of the last water distribution date, and inform all members. Through IWUGs, revised requirement requests are then sent to RIO, which regulates the amount of water available at a canal. Together with WUGs and community leaders, IWUGs fix the date for the last water distribution, which is then approved by JMC. *After* each major crop season, problems and concerns are jointly identified and crop season operations assessed through the established structure – WUGs, IWUGs, JMC. Solutions are identified in general meetings and approved by JMC.

Contrary to previous arrangements, PIM recognizes co-management between farmers (WUGs and IWUGs) and government agency (RID/RIO) at all levels of the irrigation system. Through active participation, 'individual farmers can make...joint decision[s] on water allocation, water distribution, and maintenance [of] a ditch and a canal with a WUG chief who...serves as committee member of a [IWUG]'[212]. Meetings between IWUGs and RIO are held once a month or sooner to address urgent issues. Information is announced to farmers at the WUG level through announcements via loudspeakers in the village, radio programmes, notifications and discussed at general meetings[213]. Moreover, discussions held at meetings at any of the three levels (WUGs, IWUGs, and JMC) provide opportunities for farmers and government agency staff to be exposed to information, understand the issues being raised, understand the water situation and interest of every stakeholder, get updated data, raise issues and concerns, enhance a spirit of reconciliation, and freely discuss and strategize solutions on water sharing, finite water resources, as well as water delivery techniques and patterns. This in turn, among farmers, creates a sense of inclusiveness, collaboration, communal belonging, empowerment, ownership, greater knowledge, as well as a feeling of recognition and equal treatment[214].

The economic benefit to farmers owed to PIM has been significant[215]. Statistics of 2009 registered an increase in rice yield per acre of the first and second crops of 26 and 24 percent, respectively. The sugar cane crop, as well, increased 42 percent per acre. Knowledge of water delivery status provided key information that allowed for crop diversification, which led to increased income (about 40 percent)[216], which in turn allowed farmers to lower debts and buy land. The participatory mechanism also allowed farmers to address water saving schemes, which led to a savings of 10 million m^3, equivalent to a one-year supply of water for domestic use of farmers living outside the irrigation areas.

Concluding remarks

While a comparative case analysis is presented in the following chapter against elements of Fung's (2006)[217] 'democracy cube' and issues of democratic governance, the experiences of water management in rural India and Thailand clearly confirm, even if not pervasive country-wide, that substantial benefits can be borne from meaningfully engaging citizen in both decision-making and public service delivery. As evidenced by both cases, political will and statutory protection of decentralized governance are the underlying factors contributing to raising the role of citizens to participatory stakeholders from merely service recipients. Within this backdrop, in direct response to the second research question, substantial outcomes materialized from meaningful citizen engagement in the selected countries. Positive outcomes were registered in the form of water connectivity and accessibility, improved sanitary and hygienic practices, elimination of water-borne diseases, increased income and purchasing power, increased school attendance of girls, water saving management practices, greater sense of ownership and accountability.

Chapter Four

Opportunities for citizen engagement: What factors make it effective?

Case analysis summary

The initiatives presented in Chapter Three provide an opportunity to capture commonalities, differences, as well as key principles and strategies that contributed to successful citizen engagement in rural India and Thailand. While they may not be representative country-wide, they are exemplars in their own right.

Analysis of the cases is carried out *vis-à-vis* (a) Fung's (2006)[218] 'democracy cube', (b) issues of democratic governance, and (c) factors contributing to successful outcomes. Findings are summarized in Table 1, below:

	INDIA *'Institutionalization of community managed drinking water supply programme and user level quality monitoring'*	THAILAND *'Participatory Irrigation Management'*
Reform	Decentralization at local level	Decentralization at local level
Year introduced	2004	2004
Characteristic	Participatory decision-making and service delivery	Participatory decision-making and service delivery

Participant selection	Self-selected; Selectively recruited	Self-selected; Selectively recruited
Communication and decision	Aggregation and bargaining; Deliberation and negotiation	Aggregation and bargaining; Deliberation and negotiation
Authority and power	Direct authority; Co-governing partnership	Direct authority; Co-governing partnership
Legitimacy	73rd Constitutional Amendment	1997 Constitution; 2003 Governance Reform Royal Decree
Justice	Villagers are fully informed; Influence agenda and decision making (which is finite at *gram panchayat* level)	Farmers are fully informed; Influence agenda and decision making (which is finite at JMC level)
Effectiveness	Increased household tap water connectivity; 24-hour availability; Improved sanitary/hygienic practices; Complete elimination water-borne diseases; Poverty alleviation; Reduced child mortality and morbidity; Increased income; Nearly 100% enrollment/ attendance of school age girls	Crop yields increased; More major crops carried out; Income increased; Debts reduced; New land acquired; Water savings achieved
Enabling factors to effective citizen engagement	Institutional framework change; Institutional cultural change; Capacity building; Awareness campaigns	Institutional framework change; Institutional cultural change; Capacity building; Awareness campaigns

Democracy cube analysis

Fung (2006)[219] argues '[t]here are three important dimensions along which mechanisms of participation vary'. They comprise the scope of participation (who participates), the mode of communication and decision (how – venues and means), and the extent of authority and power (what linkage is there between discussion and action).

Participant selection

Fung (2006)[220] identifies five mechanisms of popular participation. These mechanisms comprise those which are open to all (self-selected participants); those open to selectively recruited participants who have special interests in specific issues; those open to randomly selected participants, *i.e.* deliberative polling, citizen juries, planning cells; those open to unpaid lay stakeholders who have 'deep interest in some public concern and are thus willing to invest substantial time and energy to represent and serve those with similar interests or perspectives but choose not to participate'; and those open to paid professional stakeholders involved in regulatory negotiations, grassroots environmental management, and collaborative planning.

When reviewing the cases against this first dimension, findings indicate that for both potable and irrigation water systems in rural India and Thailand, respectively, participation of villagers and farmers falls under the first two characterizations – *self-selected* and *selectively recruited*. In India, findings indicate that *self-selected* villagers, from well-to-do down to the lower caste families alike, and selectively recruited representatives of the village assemblies (*gram panchayats*) have an active stake in the planning, operation, maintenance, monitoring and evaluation of drinking water supply and quality. They also make joint decisions on what technical structures are required. Similarly, as per the case in Thailand, farmers are categorized as *self-selected* (farmers members of WUGs) and *selectively recruited* (non-members of WUGs, elected representatives of IWUGs and JMC). Farmers have the opportunity to actively participate in all phases of the irrigation water management such as planning, operation, maintenance, monitoring and evaluation and make joint decisions on water allocation, water distribution, and maintenance of ditches and canals. There are also instances where non-WUG members are called to settle differences regarding abuse of WUG ditches and invited to join or form a WUG[221].

Communication and decision-making

Within the preceding mechanisms, participants have the opportunity to exert various levels of communication and decision-making engagement[222]. These range from simple spectator to technical expert. In between, there are four more degrees of participation, covering those who express preferences, develop preferences, bargain to advance aggregative preferences, and those who deliberate and negotiate solutions.

When reviewing the cases against this second dimension, findings indicate that for both cases villagers and farmers are quite active in *bargaining to advance aggregative preferences* as well as *deliberating and negotiating solutions* in general meetings at the village level (*gram sabhas*) in India and at the levels of WUG, IWUG, and JMC in Thailand. In both cases, villagers and farmers have an opportunity to exercise voice, reflect on their needs, resolve conflicts, and carry social audits. These opportunities create in villagers and farmers a sense of inclusiveness, collaboration, communal belonging, empowerment, ownership, greater knowledge, as well as a feeling of recognition and equal treatment.

Authority and power

As a third dimension, Fung (2006)[223] argues that participants may exert various degrees of authority and power. These include participants that engage for personal benefit; participate to mobilize public opinion and influence state actors; provide advice and consultation; join government officials in co-governing partnerships; and lastly, exercise direct authority over public decisions and resources.

When reviewing the cases against this third dimension, findings indicate that for both cases villagers and farmers participate in meetings to *influence* members about needed constructions, village action plans, and differential tariff schemes in India, while in Thailand on specific water irrigation requirements. Both *gram panchayats* in India and JMCs in Thailand have finite and *direct authority* over all potable water supply and quality and irrigation water management matters, respectively, through strong *co-governing partnerships* with WASMO and RID, respectively, where both entities act as technical advisors.

Democratic governance issues

'In the community of nations, governance is considered "good" and "democratic" to the degree in which a country's institutions and processes are transparent...Good governance promotes equity, participation, pluralism, transparency, accountability and the rule of law, in a manner that is effective, efficient and enduring...Democratic governance...ensures that civil society plays an active role in setting priorities and making the needs of the most vulnerable people in society known'[224]. Within this context, Fung (2006)[225] highlights issues of legitimacy, justice, and effectiveness as pillars of democratic governance.

Legitimacy

Fung (2006)[226] argues that 'public policy or action is legitimate when citizen have good reasons to support or obey it.'

When reviewing the cases against the issue of legitimacy, findings indicate that the institutional legitimacy on all matters concerning potable and irrigation water systems clearly stems from constitutional and institutional authority. In India, the 73rd Constitutional Amendment provides at the national level guarantees for citizen engagement with full discretionary authority down to the lowest level of local governance, *i.e.* the *gram panchayats* (village assemblies). In Thailand, the participatory irrigation management stems from the 1997 Constitution and the 2003 Governance Reform Royal Decree, and is part of RID's Strategic Plan, connoting, therefore, full legitimacy both at the constitutional and the government agency level. All matters discussed within the context of PIM at WUG, IWUG, and JMC meetings take place within this constitutional and institutional legitimacy.

Justice

Fung (2006)[227] argues that the lack of justice 'often results from political inequality. When some groups cannot influence the political agenda, decision-making, or gain information…because they are excluded, unorganized, or too weak, they are likely to be ill served by laws and policies.' Osmani (2008)[228] contextualizes such problems of 'systematic asymmetries of power that [are] inherent in unequal societies' as '*power gap*'.

When reviewing the cases against the issue of injustice, findings indicate that in the institutional set up in both cases villagers and farmers actively participate, are fully and timely informed, are able to influence agenda at structured meetings, and they hold decision-making authority – which is finite at the *gram panchayats* and the JMC levels – on all matters concerning potable and irrigation water management.

Effectiveness

With regards to effectiveness, Fung (2006)[229] argues that '[e]ven when public decisions are just and legitimate, state agencies may be incapable of implementing those decisions.'

When reviewing the cases against the issue of effectiveness, findings indicate that the discretionary and legitimate authority bequeathed to both *gram panchayats* and the JMCs in India and Thailand, respectively, has enabled villagers and farmer to be conduits in achieving outcomes that previous set ups in either country were never able to produce. As per the case in India, WASMO was set up precisely to address, in a decentralized manner, pressing issues of clean water accessibility and availability in rural areas. A village-centered approach provided increased household level tap water connectivity, 24-hour water availability, improved sanitary and hygienic practices, complete elimination of water-borne diseases, poverty alleviation, reduction in child mortality and morbidity, increased income, and nearly 100% enrollment and attendance of school age girls. Similarly, as per the case in Thailand, PIM was instituted specifically to address the lack of capacity and capability of RID to adequately satisfy irrigation water needs. Through a farmer-centered approach, crop yields increased substantially, two major crops are now normally carried out, income increased, debts reduced, new land has been acquired, and water savings has been achieved.

Factors contributing to successful citizen engagement

So what underlying factors contributed to making these initiatives effective? The review identifies four enabling factors to effective citizen engagement in both cases – (i) institutional framework change (decentralization), (ii) institutional cultural change, (iii) capacity building (both at institutional and community levels), and (iv) awareness campaigns.

Decentralization

Decentralization is seen as a means to 'break the grip of central government and induce broader participation in democratic governance'[230]. Gurgur and Shah (2000)[231] argue '[t]here is a general agreement in the literature that [decentralization] can open up greater opportunities for voice and choice thereby making the public sector more responsive and accountable to citizens-voters.' This is attributed to a number of underlying principles, including (i) being closer to the people, local governments are more aware of the preferences of the people; (ii) being closer to local governments, people are more aware of the works of local governments more so than the national programmes and can more directly demand services that better reflect their preferences; (iii) people can vote local officials out; and (iv) in extreme cases, people can vote with their feet.

Decentralization has played a key role in both cases in setting the stage for greater citizen engagement. In India, decentralization is protected under the arrangements of the 73rd Constitutional Amendment, which 'mandat[es] grassroots-level participation of the citizenry in development planning and implementation in rural areas, by means of village-level public meetings' known as *gram sabha*[232].

In Thailand, decentralization is protected by the 1997 Constitution and the 2003 Governance Reform Royal Decree, both of which 'recognize the rights of local communities in participating in local natural resources planning and management and demand more decentralization, transparency, and accountability in service delivery from every public agency'[233]. Both countries rely on government agencies to implement decentralized programmes – WASMO in India and RID in Thailand.

Cultural change

'[D]ecentralization does not mean that central government is not important...[To the contrary, in fact,] the government must show enough political will and commitment to be able to establish such a change'[234]. Pettigrew[235] argues that 'organizations have the capacity to transform themselves from within' and shape cultures to suit strategic ends. Fincham (2005)[236] further emphasizes that real change in organizations, if it is to occur, must take place at the cultural level, by changing organizational ethos, its image, and values. Such change must be integrated in all management processes to be effective and reflective of the spirit of the change.

Decentralization as a conceptual framework absent implementation by competent entities (both at the agency and local government levels) that enshrine the spirit of the law will undoubtedly remain ineffective. In both cases, it is precisely the political will which enabled both a change in institutional culture within the agencies and a further decentralization down to the local community level, based on strong partnerships and clearly defined roles and responsibilities.

In India, WASMO's role was, since its inception, envisaged as a facilitator rather than a provider, with the objective to 'facilitate... rural communities to carry out the implementation and bring in administrative reforms for promoting transparency, accountability, equity and responsiveness in public service'[237]. This approach contrasts with previous efforts in water management, which were captured by dominant engineers, who more than anything saw the 'hiring of fresh [experts in social sciences] for community mobilization...[as] an encroachment in their field'[238]. WASMO transformed itself into a multidisciplinary enabler, staffed 'with professionals from engineering, social sciences, environmental sciences, communications..., documentation, and management and finance'[239].

In Thailand, born from necessity – *i.e.* competition over water resources for the agricultural sector, as the country's largest consumer of water albeit the smallest contributor to the national GDP[240] – RID realized that efficient and effective water resources required bold action. This meant changing its practices to qualitative-oriented approaches to facilitate irrigation efficiency[241], whereby water decision-making of the entire irrigation system was devolved to WUGs, IWUGS, and JMC while RID serves on a technical advisory capacity only[242].

Capacity building

While several definitions exist, capacity development can be broadly defined as 'the process through which individuals, organizations and societies obtain, strengthen and maintain the capabilities to set and achieve their own development objectives over time'[243].

It is now widely acknowledged that 'lack of State capacity is...the source of many problems that developing countries face today. On the one hand, a State capacity deficit can refer [*inter alia*] to poorly managed public institutions;...[and lack] of knowledge, skills, motivation and commitment...On the other, it also relates to [the State's in]ability to create an enabling environment for...full participation of civil society in policy-making processes'[244].

In light of the above, both WASMO and RID concentrated their efforts on developing capacities and fostering attitudinal changes not only in villagers and farmers, respectively, but also in their staff through training programmes, workshops, seminars, and study tours. This approach resulted in the empowerment and strengthening of both local governance institutions and the rural community.

In India, 'WASMO...believes in investing time and resources for building capacities of each partner and stakeholder' at the community, state, and WASMO levels[245]. Recognizing its continuing nature, capacity building is provided at the pre-construction, construction, and post-construction stages of potable water management systems, covering areas like collective action and understanding, group dynamics, technical know-how, construction and financial monitoring, record keeping, water quality, personal hygiene, as well as operation and maintenance[246]. Capacity building is implemented through repeated training on developing leadership competence at the village level, classroom training, demonstrations, hands-on training, and visits to other villages. WASMO also finds it critical to develop capacities of implementing entities (NGOs) on 'participatory approach, having a dialogue with the community..., identify[ing] field issues that [require attention, as well as e]nabling the technical team to draw the design layout of [the] water supply system as per the requirements of the community and prepare village scheme[s]'[247].

In Thailand, to clarify policies, purposes, and approaches, RID carried out training sessions to all of its staff and local parties, including farmers, and advertised through publications, public meetings, and announcements[248]. RID instituted a three-year capacity building programme for its own staff to 'readjust...organizational values and cultures', *i.e.* their uncooperative attitude, and included capacity building research projects targeted at the local population to seek joint solutions for community problems[249]. The aim of the capacity building was to sensitize staff to local concerns and learn to *listen* as well as sensitize farmers about PIM (through training, study tours, meetings) and to learn to *talk and be heard*[250]. A 'sound PIM...could not be implemented without dedicated action. From the outset, field staff...tirelessly worked with farmers to form potential WUGs, IWUGS, and JMC'[251]. On the other side of the coin, PIM required the will on the part of participant farmers. This was achieved through capacity building activities that focused on awareness about PIM and all stakeholders' role and opportunities, through meetings and deliberations. This created a sense of ownership and meaningful participation[252].

Awareness campaigns

Shared by both cases, a fourth recognized enabling factor is the focused implementation of awareness campaigns.

In India, the aim of the campaigns was to promote decentralization, mobilize the community and generate awareness of WASMO and its activities, including capacity building activities for making informed decisions about water system technology options, as well as addressing challenges and barriers to hygiene and sanitation practices[253]. 'Buy-in' tailored campaigns were devised to capture the non-homogeneous nature of the communities, as different approaches and media are required to address the elderly and the youngsters, men and women, higher and lower socio-economic groups, as well as different occupational and caste groups[254]. Awareness campaigns relied on billboards, brochures, leaflets, booklets, magazines, posters, stickers, radio programmes, television, street theatre, folk-form storytelling and songs, skits and plays in schools, fairs, campaigns and drives, and video conferencing[255].

In Thailand, the experience on information dissemination is a bit more reserved and on a lesser scale and scope when compared to WASMO's approach in India. Nonetheless, the intended impact was achieved just as well, especially because never before was the community privy to information on irrigation water management. Under RID's approach, findings indicate that farmers 'regularly receive...both basic and updated water information including: the total amount of water in the...[r]eservoir; how much water could be used; how much water would be needed for the agricultural sector per crop season as well as for other relevant sectors; and how much water could be saved if the agricultural sector applied water delivery on a rotational basis'[256]. This type of information is regularly distributed at general WUG, IWUG, and JMC meetings and through bi-weekly newsletters, village loudspeaker announcements, and radio programmes at local stations. These activities became opportunities for strengthening in all stakeholders a sense of ownership, empowerment, as well as an understanding of reservoirs as finite water resources and relationship among saving water, the next crop season water requirements, and multiple crops per season[257].

Concluding remarks

Contrary to conventional wisdom[258], evidence from the cases presented above provides a positive example of meaningful citizen engagement notwithstanding the level of democratic maturity of either country. Both cases have very much in common, including enjoying political will and statutory authority, commitment to capacity building of both institutional staff and local communities, as well as an active public awareness campaign. These four elements have made water management in rural India and Thailand a successful example of citizen engagement in public governance both at the decision-making and implementation levels.

Chapter Five

Conclusion and Recommendations

Conclusion

Citizens do not feel empowered and do not feel they are adequately given the space to meaningfully participate in public governance. Clearly, citizens are not satisfied with the manner in which government is run. This is evident across the developed and developing world, as highlighted also by recent manifestation of discontent in Europe, North America, North Africa, the Middle East, and Asia.

A key way to ensure that government truly reflects the will of the people, particularly the marginalized and the weaker groups of society, is by creating an environment where citizens are given democratic space to exercise '*voice*'. Participatory governance is key to development and to the improvement in the lives of people. By no means is this research advocating against the centrality of government in society, to the contrary. The disenchantment with strict representative democracy, however, reinforces the fact that a continuum should and can exist where citizens are given the opportunity to meaningfully have a say in policy decisions and implementation even in between elections.

Within this context, the research set out to answer two questions – (i) *What major factors account for greater citizen engagement in policy making and public service delivery?* (ii) *In what ways does citizen engagement in public governance matter?*

With regards to the first question, the research addressed two of the leading trends worldwide that contribute to greater citizen engagement in public governance – (i) the paradigmatic shift in public administration from the 'managerialism' of the New Public Management (NPM) to the 'inclusiveness' of Public Value Management (PVM), and (ii) the demand for a shift from representative to participatory democracy.

With the exception of a *disegual* weight on outputs, NPM and PVM share little similarities. While the former has been heavily criticized for running government like a business relegating individuals to the role of beneficiaries of services provided, the latter recognizes, instead, the centrality of individuals in participatory decision-making and public service delivery. Also, while NPM focuses on efficiency and economization (which remain essential in the works of government), such principles should not be construed as government's ultimate goal, but rather simply a means to an end. This 'end' is clearly captured by the principles of PVM, for it recognizes the role of citizens as shapers of their own welfare. Citizen engagement itself, however, should not be regarded the ultimate goal but simply a means to achieve outcomes that address citizens needs as citizens see them rather than how they are perceived or imposed by elected officials.

The other leading trend covered that accounts for greater citizen engagement is the revitalization of democratic principles. Representative democracy does not fulfill the needs and will of citizens because, in between elections, every-day decisions that affect their lives are not taken by the citizens themselves but rather by elected officials. For this reason, citizens around the world have grown dissatisfied with the way government is run. This dissatisfaction is evidenced by the decreasing citizen participation in political parties and voting turnout in elections. The research also captured a number of examples highlighting how citizen involvement in decision-making contributed to national policy changes leading to better access to public goods and housing in Brazil, budget reforms on maternal mortality in Mexico, land reforms in the Philippines, recognition of HIV/AIDS as a health issue in South Africa, and increased income for the working poor in the United States.

To address the second question, the research focused on water management in rural Asia. There are a number of reasons for this geographical focus – (i) Asia is the most populous continent in the world, (ii) 58 percent of its population resides in rural areas, and (iii) waterborne diseases kill millions and affect billions. More particularly, the research focused on India and Thailand, whose rural population account for 70 percent and 66 percent, respectively. Rural population is tendentially weaker and more marginalized than the urban population. What was interesting about India and Thailand was the challenges citizen engagement has traditionally endured in these countries. Democratically, India is regarded a consolidated democracy, nonetheless qualitative citizen engagement has been hampered by high illiteracy across the country as well as structurally embedded socioeconomic inequalities (castes, sub-castes, tribes). Thailand was particularly selected because its democratization has been curtailed by a junta regime since a *coup d'etates* in 2006. Even more markedly than the experience in India, democracy in Thailand is culturally conditioned by fundamental inequalities that derive from the proximity of an individual to the monarchy.

Under a hierarchical system, Thai people know their place in society (subservient to superiors) in a country where the aristocracy controls the instruments of power and regards the masses as a threat.

Against this unwelcoming backdrop, results borne from the active engagement of citizens in water management in rural India and Thailand assume a much more flavorful meaning. These results support the premise that citizen engagement, when properly implemented, does matter in improving the welfare of people. Fundamentally, citizen engagement in both potable water and water irrigation management in India and Thailand, respectively, was effective in creating a sense of ownership, empowerment, inclusiveness, collaboration, recognition, and equal treatment. From a tangible perspective, in India, citizen engagement contributed to increased household tap water connectivity, 24-hour water availability, improved sanitary/hygienic practices, complete elimination of water-borne diseases, poverty alleviation, reduced child mortality and morbidity, increased income, nearly 100 percent enrollment/attendance of school age girls. In Thailand, benefits resulted in increased crop yields, increased number of major yearly crops carried out, increased income, reduced debt, new land acquisitions, and water savings. These results are a strong reflection of how citizen engagement matters in public governance and how it can make a difference in the lives of people.

What is also quite interesting about the findings is that successful strategies implemented by the both Indian and Thai governments were built upon political will, statutory protection of decentralized governance, commitment to capacity building of both institutional staff and local communities, as well as an active public awareness campaign. These are the factors that have rendered citizen engagement in decision-making and public service delivery in rural India and

Thailand a success, carrying with them potential for replication, in spite of the democratic context characterizing the two countries.

Recommendations

Fung (2006)[259] argues 'there is no canonical form of direct participation in modern democratic governance'. The same can then be said for factors contributing towards effective citizen engagement. While it is true one size does not fit all and while we should steer away from attempting to adopt a successful exogenous policy without adapting it to local conditions, there appears to be an almost identical approach when water management systems are compared in rural India and Thailand. Can we then conclude that the four-pronged approach – decentralization, cultural change, capacity building, and awareness campaign – adopted and adapted by WASMO and RID is typical of water management systems? While the answer to this question is outside the scope of this research, we certainly should neither regard this approach the only approach available nor limited to the water sector only. Analyzing what worked elsewhere is only but a first step towards a more strategic approach that enables and encourages citizen engagement. And what worked elsewhere can potentially be adapted elsewhere. With this in mind, there is room for the replication of the four-pronged approach as it is based on principles that are intuitively sound. That said, and drawing from operational principles highlighted by both cases, the following is recommended in order to promote and safeguard the meaningful participation of citizens in governance.

The government has the responsibility to create an environment that enables the full expression of citizen engagement. To this end, while not limited to, the government should:

- *Legitimize decentralization* – Citizen engagement should constitute a civil right protected by the constitution. From this point, decentralization should not be limited to the creation of independent and self-reliant government agencies alone but, rather, it should be further extended to local communities.

- *Institutionalize cultural change* – Decentralization should not merely be a paper or cosmetic exercise. In order for decentralization to truly work as intended, there needs to be a change management approach within the government. Devoid of political will, commitment, and attitude on the part of the government, decentralization will not fare positively.

- *Promote capacity development* – Decentralization without capacity will be ineffective. As it would not make any sense to transfer authority and powers to local communities, whose competence is not commensurate to the job at hand and responsibilities required, capacity development is essential. This requires focused and tailored capacity development activities, – *e.g.* training programmes, workshops, seminars, and study tours – for both government staff and communities. This approach creates a sense of inclusiveness, collaboration, communal belonging, empowerment, ownership, greater knowledge, as well as a feeling of recognition and equal treatment.

- *Promote awareness* – There is nothing less effective than to have a good idea and not advertise it. Information is key at all levels and should be easily accessible. The government should conduct 'buy-in' tailored campaigns that address the non-homogeneous nature of communities and rely on billboards, brochures, leaflets, booklets, magazines, posters, stickers, radio programmes, television, fairs, campaigns and drives, and video conferencing, as well as local traditional activities.

A fundamental principle of citizen engagement is that of 'pro-activity'. Citizen engagement will never work if citizens themselves are passive and do not take advantage of enabling environments granted by the government. In this regard, citizens should actively:

- *Get involved* – While nothing happens before its time, citizens must get involved in order for change to happen. While it is recognized 'that participation in public affairs is not costless'[260], there is nothing stronger than the exponential power of unity, in number and purpose.

- *Get organized* – Citizen should establish a clear mandate and should get organize in such a way to ensure the message is clear, coherent, and fully supported among constituents[261].

- *Promote demand driven initiatives* – This means making the issue known and well publicized to the government and fellow citizens. It means advertising the issue through the same media noted above under 'Promote awareness'.

- *Ensure inclusiveness* – Excluding and marginalizing weaker people in society is reprehensible. It is unacceptable when governments do that, the more if citizens or citizen groups practice the same.

- *Strengthen own capacities* – As argued by Osmani (2008)[262], 'meaningful participation…requires certain skills which common people, least of all traditionally disadvantaged and marginalized segments of society, do not typically possess.' It is therefore essential for citizens to create conditions for themselves that would facilitate the natural transfer of authority and power from the government. Decentralizing for the sake of decentralizing will not be as effective as when granted to competent citizens.

Concluding remarks

In fine, while government is indeed central to society, partnerships and co-decision-making management arrangements can work well as illustrated by the cases in India and Thailand. Citizens see their engagement in the democratic process necessary to reaffirm and safeguard democratic values and dialogue, their meaningful role in governance, and the values that best serve public interest. Citizens want to have '*voice*' in affairs that matter to them the most. Citizen engagement embodies a golden opportunity, for once, to 'do the right thing' *by* and *for* society at large on matters citizens rather than elected representatives deem of value. After all, it is 'the man who wears the shoe [rather than the shoemaker,] who knows best that it pinches and where it pinches'[263].

ENDNOTES

Chapter One - Introduction

1 Smith and Wales, 2000; Oakley, 2002; Bouras *et al.*, 2003 Noordhoek and Saner, 2004; Welch *et al.*, 2004; Cooper *et al.*, 2006, cited in Yetano, Royo, and Acerete, 2009, p.2
2 Zipfel and Gaventa, 2008, p.2
3 *ibid.*, 2008, p.1
4 Cornwall and Gaventa, 2001, p.iii
5 United Nations, 2007
6 cited in Blair, 2008, p.77
7 Setala, 2008, p.151
8 United Nations, 1986
9 United Nations, 1966
10 Bourgon, 2007
11 Goetz and Gaventa, 2001, p.5
12 *ibid.*, 2001, p.1
13 Bourgon, 2007
14 Bourgon, 2008, p.398
15 Shin, 2008, p.1
16 *ibid.*, p.3
17 Huntington, 1993; Bell, 2006; Bell *et al.*, 1995; Compton, 2000; Pye, 1997; Tu, 1996, cited in Shin, 2008, p.3
18 Shin, 2008, p.3
19 United Nations, 2011b
20 World Health Organization, 2011
21 United Nations, 2009
22 World Bank, 2009a
23 World Bank, 2009b
24 Fung, 2006
25 Bhattacharyya, 2006, p.40

26 Albritton and Bureekul, 2008, pp.20-21

Chapter Two – Citizen engagement in public governance: Challenges and trends

27 Fung, p.17

28 Bourgon, 2009, p.3

29 Bourgon, 2008

30 Fung, p.17

31 *ibid.*

32 Metcalfe, 1989, cited in Yamamoto, 2003, p.3

33 Batley and Larby, 2004, cited in Haque, 2007, p.180

34 Stoker, 2006, p.46

35 *ibid.*, p.47

36 Hood and Peters, 2004, p.267

37 *ibid.*, p.271

38 Hoggett, 1996; Hood *et al.*, 1999; Jones and Thompson, 1999; Light, 1993, cited in Hood and Peters, 2004, p.271

39 Denhardt and Denhardt, 2000, p.549

40 Dunleavy *et al.*, 2005, p.477

41 *ibid.*

42 Minogue, 2000, cited in O'Flynn, 2007, p.357

43 Stoker, 2006, p.53

44 *ibid.*, p.52

45 *ibid.*, p.50

46 Liegl, 1998, p.15

47 Vabo, 2009, p.2

48 Liegl, 1998, p.17

49 OECD, 2003, cited in O'Flynn, 2007, pp.357-358

50 O'Flynn, 2007, p.359

51 *ibid.*

52 Stoker, 2006, p.50

53 Minogue, 2000, cited in O'Flynn, 2007, p.357

54 Drechsler, 2005, cited in Vabo, 2009, p.5

55 Stoker, 2006, p.49

56 Dibben, Wood, and Roper, 2004, cited in Haque, 2007, p.182

57 Vigoda, 2002, p.534

58 Pollitt, 1995, cited in Yamamoto, 2003, p.8

59 Denhardt and Denhardt, 2000, p.555

60 Argyriades, 2003, p.16

61 Yamamoto, 2003, p.6

62 Haque, 2009, pp.12-13

63 Fountain, 2001, p.64

64 *ibid.*, p.56

65 Argyriades, 2003, p.16

66 Fountain, 2001, pp.67-69

67 *ibid.*, p.56

68 Dalton, Burklin, and Drumond, 2001, p.142

69 *ibid.*

70 Setala, pp.151-152

71 May, 1978, cited in Budge, 2005

72 Debicka and Debicki, 2006

73 *ibid.*

74 Bourgon, 2007

75 Budge, 2005

76 Merton, 1940, p.563

77 Debicka and Debicki, 2006

78 Becker and Ravelson, 2008, p.20

79 Debicka and Debicki, 2006

80 Becker and Ravelson, 2008, p.20

81 Kabeer, 2003, cited in Gaventa and Barrett, 2010, p.33

82 Friedman, 2010, cited in Gaventa and Barrett, 2010, pp.34,36

83 Gaventa and Mayo, 2009, cited in Gaventa and Barrett, 2010, p.34

84 Borras and Franco, 2010, cited in Gaventa and Barrett, 2010, p.34

85 *ibid.* pp.34,36

86 Avritzer, 2010, cited in Gaventa and Barrett, 2010, p.36

87 Layton *et al.*, 2010, cited in Gaventa and Barrett, 2010, p.36

88 Barnes, 2007, cited in Gaventa and Barrett, 2010, p.37

89 Luce, 2006, cited in Gaventa and Barrett, 2010, p.37

90 Cornwall and Gaventa, 2001, p.3

91 *ibid.*, p.4

92 United Nations, 2008, p.23

93 Stiglitz, 1998, cited in Gaventa and McGee, 2010, p.7

94 Ginsburg, 2007, p.2

95 Stiglitz, 1998, cited in Gaventa and McGee, 2010, p.7

96 Barber, 1984, quoted in Fung, 2007, p.450

97 *ibid.*

98 United Nations, 1996, p.26

99 Adam, 1997, cited in Karini, 2008, p.5

100 United Nations, 1996, p.26

101 Sadashiva, 2010, p.8

102 Suri, 2008, p.11

103 Bhattacharyya, 2006, p.40

104 Wasi, cited in Albritton and Bureekul, 2008, p.20

105 Albritton and Bureekul, 2008, p.20

106 *ibid.*, 2008, p.21

107 Noordhoek and Saner, 2004; Oakley, 2002, cited in Yetano, Royo, and Acerete, 2009, p.2

108 Nye, 1997; Muts and Flemming, 1999; Peters, 1999, cited in Yetano, Royo, and Acerete, 2009, p.2

109 Bourgon, 2007

110 *ibid.*

Chapter Three - Valuing citizens in policy making and public service delivery

[111] Redford, 1969, cited in Denhardt and Denhardt, 2011a, p.51
[112] Denhardt and Denhardt, 2011a, p.114
[113] Cooper, 1991, quoted in Denhardt and Denhardt, 2011a, p.114
[114] Osmani, 2008, p.2
[115] Denhardt and Denhardt, 2011a, p.172
[116] Lucio, 2009, cited in Denhardt and Denhardt, 2011a, p.172
[117] Denhardt and Denhardt, 2011a, p.172
[118] *ibid.*
[119] Osmani, 2008, p.4
[120] Goetz and Gaventa, 2001, p.9
[121] Suri, 2008, p.1
[122] Sharma, 2002, cited in Sadashiva, 2010, p.4
[123] Sadashiva, 2010, p.4
[124] Mandelbaum, 1970; World Lingo, 2010, cited in Sadashiva, 2010, p.5
[125] Suri, 2008, p.4
[126] *ibid.*, p.5
[127] Sadashiva, 2010, p.5
[128] Government of India, 2001, cited in Sadashiva, 2010, p.5
[129] Sadashiva, 2010, p.5
[130] *ibid.*, p.10
[131] DIT, 2011, p.3
[132] Bhattacharyya, 2006, p.40
[133] *ibid.*, p.44
[134] India Code, 2010, cited in Sadashiva, 2010, p.6
[135] Sadashiva, 2010, p.11
[136] World Bank, 2009
[137] Sadashiva, 2010, p.12
[138] WASMO, 2008, p.121
[139] United Nations, 2011b, p.186

[140] WASMO, 2009b

[141] WASMO, 2008, p.1

[142] One World Foundation, 2011, p.3

[143] WASMO, 2009c, pp.1-2

[144] WASMO, 2008, p.8

[145] Reynders and Ahmed, 2005, p.162

[146] WASMO, 2009c, p.2

[147] WASMO, 2008, p.8

[148] WASMO, 2009a

[149] WASMO, 2009c, p.2

[150] WASMO, 2009a

[151] WASMO, 2008, p.8

[152] WASMO, 2009c, p.2

[153] WASMO, 2009a

[154] Reynders and Ahmed, 2005, p.164

[155] WASMO, 2008, p.17

[156] *ibid.*, p.38

[157] GSDWICL, 2000, quoted in Reynders and Ahmed, 2005, p.163

[158] WASMO, 2008, p.10

[159] WASMO, 2009a

[160] WASMO, 2011

[161] WASMO, 2009b

[162] *ibid.*

[163] WASMO, 2008, p.38

[164] WASMO, 2009b

[165] WASMO, 2008, pp.43,46

[166] *ibid.*, p.20

[167] WASHCost, 2009

[168] WASMO, 2011

[169] WASMO, 2008, p.47

[170] *ibid.*, p.7

[171] *ibid.*, p.42

[172] WASMO, 2009b

[173] *ibid.*

[174] Parikh, 2009, p.2

[175] WASMO, 2009b

[176] Parikh, 2009, p.3

[177] Albritton and Bureekul, 2008, pp.1-2

[178] Orlandini, 2003, p.108

[179] Amara, 1999, cited in Orlandini, 2003, p.109

[180] Orlandini, 2003, p.129

[181] 2001, cited in Orlandini, 2003, p.111

[182] Orlandini, 2003, p.111

[183] *ibid.*, pp.89-90

[184] Albritton and Bureekul, 2008, pp.8-9

[185] Sattayanurak, 2007, cited in Albritton and Bureekul, 2008, p.10

[186] *ibid.*, p.12

[187] Albritton and Bureekul, 2008, p.21

[188] Fisher, 2001; Argiros, 2001, cited in Orlandini, 2003, p.125

[189] NBS, 2011

[190] United Nations, 2011b, p.42

[191] Kumnerdpet, 2010, p.iv

[192] RID, 2011a

[193] Kumnerdpet, 2010, p.3

[194] Ounvichit and Satoh, 2002, cited in Kumnerdpet, 2010, p.104

[195] Hoynck and Rieser, 2002, cited in Kumnerdpet, 2010, p.104

[196] Molle, Ngernprasertsri, and Sudsawasd, 2002, cited in Kumnerdpet, 2010, p.104

[197] *ibid.*, p.121

[198] RDI, 2011a

[199] Sirisumphand, 2011

[200] Sagardoy, Bottrall, and Uittenbogaard, 1982, cited in Kumnerdpet, 2010, p.79

[201] RID, 2011a

[202] Informant No.34, quoted in Kumnerdpet, 2010, p.114

[203] Rattanatangtrakul, 2007

204 NBS, 2011

205 Phupa cited in NBS, 2011

206 RID, 2011b

207 Kumnerdpet, 2010, pp.86-98

208 RID, 2005, cited in Kumnerdpet, 2010, p.92

209 *ibid.*, p.96

210 Kumnerdpet, 2010, pp.92-97

211 *ibid.*, p.107

212 RID, 2005, cited in Kumnerdpet, 2010, p.109

213 Kumnerdpet, 2010, pp.109-110

214 *ibid.*, pp.159,175,177,195,201

215 Pureesrisak, 2011

216 noted by Sirisumphand, 2011

217 Fung, 2006

218 *ibid.*

Chapter Four – Opportunities for citizen engagement: What factors make it effective?

219 Fung, 2006, p.1

220 *ibid.*, pp. 5-7

221 Kumnerdpet, 2010, p.141

222 Fung, 2006, pp.8-11

223 *ibid.*, pp.11-13

224 United Nations, 2011a

225 Fung, 2006

226 *ibid.*, p.14

227 *ibid.*, p.16

228 Osmani, 2008, p.31

229 Fung, 2006, p.20

230 Olowy, 2000; Smoke, 1994; Wunsch and Olowu, 1990, cited in Fjeldstad, 2004, p.1

231 Gurgur and Shah, 2000, p.4

232 Sadashiva, 2010, p.6

233 Kumnerdpet, 2010, p.83

234 Becker and Ravelson, 2008, p.18

235 cited in Fincham, 2005

236 Fincham, 2005

237 WASMO, 2009a

238 *ibid.*

239 *ibid.*

240 Kumnerdpet, 2010, p.82

241 *ibid.*, p.83

242 *ibid.*, p.176

243 UNDP, 2007

244 United Nations, 2005, p.4

245 WASMO, 2008, p.31

246 *ibid.*, p.32

247 *ibid.*, p.34

248 Kumnerdpet, 2010, pp.99-100

249 *ibid.*, pp.117-118,125

250 *ibid.*, pp.119-120

251 *ibid.*, p.173

252 *ibid.*, pp.126-127

253 WASMO, 2008, p.22

254 *ibid.*

255 *ibid.*, pp.23-29

256 Kumnerdpet, 2010, pp.207-208

257 *ibid.*, p.208

258 Gaventa and Barrett, 2010, p.54

[259] Fung, 2006, p.2

[260] Osmani, 2008

[261] IDS, 2006, p.4

[262] *ibid.*

[263] Dewey, 1927, quoted in Schutz, 2001, p.301

REFERENCES

Albritton, R. and Bureekul, T. (2008) 'The state of democracy in Thailand' [online] www.asianbarometer.org/newenglish/publications/conferencepapers/2008conference/sec.3.2.pdf [Accessed 17 June 2011]

Argyriades, D. (2003) 'Values in public management - The Millennium Declaration: Some implications for management at the national and international levels', United Nations Thessaloniki Centre for Public Service Professionalism, *UNTC Occasional Papers Series* (2003) (2), pp.1-17

Becker, P. and Ravelon, J-A.A. (2008) 'What is democracy?' [online] library.fes.de/pdf-files/bueros/madagaskar/05860.pdf [Accessed 5 June 2011]

Bhattacharyya, R. (2006) 'Qualitative participation and social harmony: A study of the literacy movement in West Bengal (India)' [online] www.adb.org/documents/ books/role-public-administration-building-harmonious-society/session1.pdf [Accessed 17 June 2011]

Blair, H. (2008) 'Innovations in participatory local governance: An overview of issues and evidence' In United Nations *ed.* (2008) *Participatory governance and the Millennium Development Goals (MDGs)*, New York: United Nations Publications

Bourgon, J. (2009) 'New governance and public administration: Towards a dynamic synthesis' [online] jocelynbourgon.com/

documents/governance%20paper-canberra%20_feb_16 _v21%20_philley%20edits.pdf [Accessed 24 March 2011]

Bourgon, J. (2008a) 'The future of public service: A search for a new balance', *The Australian Journal of Public Administration*, vol.67 (4), pp.390-404

Bourgon, J. (2008b) 'Reclaiming public administration' [online] joycebourgon.ca/ documents/2008/2008_03_03_e.html [Accessed 17 June 2011]

Bourgon, J. (2007) 'Why should governments engage citizens in service delivery and policy making?' [online] www.oecd.org/ dtaoecd/7/51/42240216.pdf [Accessed 21 April 2011]

Budge, I. (2005) 'Direct and representative democracy' Are they necessarily opposed? [online] unpan1.un.org/intradoc/ groups/ public/documents/un/unpan021104.pdf [Accessed 10 June 2011]

Cornwall, A. and Gaventa, J. (2001) 'From users and choosers to makers and shapers: Repositioning participant in social policy', Institute of Development Studies, IDS Working Paper 127 [online] www.ids.ac.uk/go/ids publication/from-users-and-choosers-to-makers-and-shapers-repositioning-participant-in-social-policy [Accessed on 20 June 2011]

Dalton, R.J., Burklin, W., and Drummond, A. (2001) 'Public opinion and direct democracy', *Journal of Democracy*, vol.12 (4) October 2001, pp.141-153

Debicka, A. and Debicki, M. (2006) 'Public service and the democratic deficit' [online] unpan1.un.org/intradoc/groups/ public/ nispacee/unpan021402.pdf [Accessed 10 June 2011]

Denhardt, J.V. and Denhardt, R.B. (2011) *The new public service: Serving, not steering*, Third editions, Armonk: M.E. Sharpe Inc.

Denhardt, R.B. and Denhardt, J.V. (2000) 'The New Public Service: Serving rather than steering', *Public Administration Review*, 2000, vol.60 (6), pp.549-559

Department of Information Technology (2011) 'Framework for citizen engagement in NeGP', Government of India [online] www.mit.gov.in/sites/upload_files/dit/files/framework_for_citizen_engagement_in_negp2_0.pdf [Accessed 25 July 2011]

Dunleavy, P., Margetts, H., Bastow, S. and Tinkler, J. (2005) 'New Public Management is dead – Long live digital-era governance', *Journal of Public Administration Research and Theory*, vol.16, pp.467-494

Fincham, R. (2005) 'Organizational culture' [online] fds.oup.com/www.oup.co.uk/pdf/bt/fincham/chapter15.pdf [Accessed 15 August 2011]

Fjeldstad, O. (2004) 'Decentralization and corruption: A review of the literature', Chr. Michelsen Institute, CMI Working Paper WP 2004:10

Fountain, J.E. (2001) 'Paradoxes of public sector customer service', *Governance: An International Journal of Policy and Administration*, vol.14 (1), January 2001, pp.55-73

Fung, A. (2007) 'Democratic theory and political science: A pragmatic method of constructive engagement', *American Political Science Review*, vol.101 (3), August 2007, pp.443-458

Fung, A. (2006) 'Varieties of participation in complex governance', [online] www.archonfung.net/papers/papers.html [Accessed 17 June 2011]

Fung, A. 'Innovations in participation: Citizen engagement in deliberative democracy' [online] www.innovations.harvard.edu/cache/documents/1030/103001.pdf [Accessed 21 April 2011]

Gaventa, J. and Barrett, G. (2010) 'So what difference does it make? Mapping the outcomes of citizen engagement' [online] http://www.drc-citizenship.org/system/assets/1052734701/original/1052734701-gaventa_etal.2010-so.pdf?1299610435 [Accessed 20 July 2011]

Gaventa, J. and McGee, R. (2010) 'Introduction: Making change happen – Citizen action and national policy reform' [online] www.drc-citizenship.org/system/assets/1052734655/original/1052734655-gaventa_etal.2010-making.pdf?1299502105 [Accessed 20 July 2011]

Ginsburg, T. (2007) 'Lessons for democratic transition: Case studies from Asia' [online] www.lexglobal.org/files/046_orbis-final.pdf [Accessed 26 June 2011]

Goetz, A.M. and Gaventa, J. (2001) 'Bringing citizen voice and client focus into service delivery', Institute of Development Studies, IDS Working Paper 138 [online] siteresources.worldbank.org / intpceng/1143372-1116506145151/20511053/wp.pdf [Accessed on 20 June 2011]

Gurgur, T. and Shah, A. (2000) 'Localization and Corruption: Panacea or Pandora's Box?' [online] www.imf.org/external/ pubs/ft/ seminar/2000/fiscal/gurgur.pdf [Accessed 12 July 2010]

Haque, M.S. (2009) 'Public administration public governance in Singapore' [online] profile.nus.edu.sg/fass/polhaque/s-haque_ singapore.pdf [Accessed 24 March 2011]

Haque, M.S. (2007) 'Revisiting the New Public Management', *Public Administration Review*, January/February 2007, pp.179-182

Haque, M.S. (2003) 'Citizen participation in governance through representation: Issues of gender in East Asia', *International Journal of Public Administration*, vol.26 (5), pp.569-590

Hood, C. and Peters, G. (2004) 'The Middle-Aging of New Public Management: Into the age of paradox?', *Journal of Public Administration Research and Theory*, vol.14 (3), pp.267-282

Institute of Development Policies – IDS (2006) 'Making space for citizens: Broadening the 'new democratic spaces' for citizen participation', IDS Policy Briefing, March 2006 (27), [online] www.drc-citizenship.org/system/asets/1052734498/original/ 1052734498-shankland.2006-making.pdf?1299612284 [Accessed 20 July 2011]

Karini, A. (2008) 'Building citizen centered policy-making', Policy Paper, Institute for Democracy and Mediation [online] idmalbania.org/publications/en/citizen_centred _policy_making.en.pdf [Accessed 17 June 2011]

Kumnerdpet, W. (2010) 'Community learning and empowerment through Participatory Irrigation Management: Case studies from Thailand' [online] umanitoba.ca/institutes/natural_resources/pdf/thesis/phd%20thesis%20kumnerdpet%202010.pdf [Accessed 28 July 2011]

Liegl, B. (1998) 'The fallacies of New Public Management - Can they still be prevented in the Austrian context?' [online] www.essex.ac.uk/ecpr/events/jointsessions/paperarchive/mannheim/w1/liegl.pdf [Accessed 24 March 2011]

Merton, R.K. (1940) 'Bureaucratic Structure and Personality', *Social Forces*, vol.18 (4), May 1940, pp.560-568

National Broadcasting Services - NBS (2011) television broadcast aired on 14 January 2011 [online] unpan3.un.org/unps/m_upload.aspx?id=941 [Accessed 26 July 2011]

O'Flynn, J. (2007) 'From New Public Management to Public Value: Pragmatic change and managerial implications' [online] wiki.douglasbastien.com/images/1/1d/from_new_public_management_to_public_value.pdf [Accessed 24 March 2011]

One World Foundation, India (2011) 'Ghogha rural drinking water supply project: Documentation of best practices' [online] indiagovernance.gov.in/download.php?filename=files/

ghogha _project_documentation[1] [Accessed 5 August 2011]

Orlandini, B. (2003) 'Civic engagement in local governance: The case of Thailand' [online] www.unpan.org/library/searchdocuments /tabid/1111/language/en-us/ default.aspx [Accessed 18 April 2011]

Osmani, S.R. (2008) 'Participatory governance: An overview of issues and evidence' In United Nations *ed.* (2008) *Participatory governance and the Millennium Development Goals (MDGs)*, Department of Economic and Social Affairs, New York: United Nations Publications

Parikh, K. (2009) Member Planning Commission Yojana Bhawan, New Delhi [online] unpan3.un.org/unps/m_upload.aspx?id =560 [Accessed 26 June 2011]

Pureesrisak, S. (2011) Governor of Suphan Buri Province, Thailand, Letter dated 1 March 2011 [online] unpan3.un.org/unps/ m_upload.aspx?id=941 [Accessed 26 July 2011]

Rattanatangtrakul, U. (2007) 'Participatory Irrigation Management (PIM) in Thailand' [online] www.rid.go.th/thaicid/_5_article /2549/07pim.pdf [Accessed 28 July 2011]

Reynders, J. and Ahmed, S. (2005) 'Who's water? Learning from public-private partnership in Gujarat' [online] www.irc.nl/ content/download/20863/249844/file/reyndersahmed.pdf [Accessed 5 August 2011]

Royal Irrigation Department, Thailand (2011a) [online] unpan3.un.org/unps/m_nominationgeneralinfo.aspx?id=941 [Accessed 26 July 2011]

Royal Irrigation Department, Thailand (2011b) 'Participatory Irrigation management by Civil Society Committee and Water User Organizations: The Kra Seaw Operation and Maintenance Office, Dan Chang District, Suphanburi Province, Thailand' [online] unpan1.un.org/intradoc /groups/public/documents/un-dpadm/unpan046058.pdf [Accessed 28 June 2011]

Royal Irrigation Department, Thailand (2011c) [online] unpan3.un.org/unps/m_upload. aspx?id=941 [Accessed 26 July 2011]

Sadashiva, M. (2010) 'Revitalizing democracy and participation in India: Recent national policy initiatives' [online] buergerstiftungen.de/cps/rde/xbcr/sid-33355975-939ab555/bst/manjunath%20sadashiva.pdf [Accessed 17 June 2011]

Setala, M. (2008) 'Representative democracy' [online] www.tampereclub.org/e-publications/vol3_setala.pdf [Accessed on 5 June 2011]

Shin, D.C. (2008) 'The Third Wave in East Asia: Comparative and dynamic perspectives' [online] www.asianbarometer.org/newenglish/publications/conferencepapers/2008conference/sec.1.1.pdf [Accessed 17 June 2011]

Sirisumphand, T. (2011) Secretary-General of the Office of the Public Sector Development Commission, Thailand, Letter dated 25 February 2011 [online] unpan3.un.org/unps/m_upload.aspx?id =941 [Accessed 26 July 2011]

Stoker, G. (2006) 'Public Value Management: A narrative for Networked Governance?', *The American Review of Public Administration*, vol.36 (1), pp.41-57

Suri, K.C. (2008) 'The state of democratic governance in India' [online] www.asianbarometer.org/newenglish/publications/conferencepapers/2008conference/sec.6.1.pdf [Accessed 17 June 2011]

Schutz, A. (2001) 'John Dewey and "a Paradox of Size": Democratic faith at the limits of experience' [online] www.education action.org/uploads/1/0/4/5/104537/dewey_paradox.pdf [Accessed 2 August 2011]

United Nations (2011a) 'Governance' [online] http://www.un.org/en/globalissues/ governance [Accessed 14 August 2011]

United Nations (2011b) Department of Economic and Social Affairs 'Good practices and innovations in public governance: United Nations Public Service Awards winners 2003-2011', New York: United Nations Publications [online] unpan1.un.org/intradoc/groups/public/documents/un/unpan046119.pdf [Accessed on 19 July 2011]

United Nations (2009) Department of Economic and Social Affairs [online] esa.un.org/unpd/wup/index.htm [Accessed 5 August 2011]

United Nations (2008) *People Matter: Civic engagement in public governance*, Department of Economic and Social Affairs, New York: United Nations Publications

United Nations (2007) Department of Economic and Social Affairs 'Institutionalizing civic engagement for building trust: The case of the Economic and Social Councils', New York: United Nations Publications

United Nations (2005) Economic and Social Council document on 'Bottom-up approaches and methodologies to develop foundations and principles public administration: The example of criteria-based organizational assessment' (E/C.16/2005/3)

United Nations (1996) General Assembly document on 'Public administration and development' (A/50/847)

United Nations (1986) General Assembly resolution on the 'Declaration on the Rights to Development' (A/RES/41/126)

United Nations (1966) General Assembly resolution on the 'International Covenant on Civil and Political Rights' (A/RES/2200A/XXI)

United Nations Development Programme (2007) [online] www.capacity.undp.org [Accessed 15 August 2011]

Vabo, M. (2009) 'New Public Management: The neoliberal way of governance' [online] www.ts.hi.is/working%20paper%204-2009.pdf [Accessed 24 March 2011]

Vigoda, E. (2002) 'From responsiveness to collaboration: Governance, citizens, and the next generation of public administration', *Public Administration Review*, vol.62 (5), pp.527-540

WASHCost (2009) 'Drastic change, but not a dream – Lessons from WASH sector in Gujarat' [online] www.washcost.info/drastic %20change%20not%20a%20dream%20–%20lessons%20 from%20wash%20sector%20in%20gujarat[1].pdf [Accessed 5 August 2011]

Water and Sanitation Management Organisation – WASMO (2011) [online] www.wasmo.org/cms.aspx? [Accessed 5 August 2011]

Water and Sanitation Management Organisation – WASMO (2009a) [online] unpan3.un.org/unps/m_nominationgeneralinfo. aspx? id =560 [Accessed 26 June 2011]

Water and Sanitation Management Organisation – WASMO (2009b) [online] unpan3.un.org/unps/m_nominationprofileprint. aspx? id=560 [Accessed 26 June 2011]

Water and Sanitation Management Organisation – WASMO (2009c) 'Water and sanitation management and surveillance programme: Institutionalization of users' level' [online] unpan3.un.org/unps/m_upload.aspx?id=560 [Accessed 26 June 2011]

Water and Sanitation Management Organisation – WASMO (2008) 'From policy to practice: Users as managers of rural drinking water supply systems' [online] www.wasmo.org/downloads / from_ policy_to_practice.pdf [Accessed 3 August 2011]

World Bank (2009a) 'Rural population (% of total population)' [online] search.worldbank.org/data?qterm=rural+population

+in+india&language=en&format= [Accessed 5 August 2011]

World Bank (2009b) 'Rural population (% of total population)' [online] search.worldbank. org/data?qterm=rural+population +in+thailand&language=en&format= [Accessed 5 August 2011]

World Health Organization (2011) 'WHO issues revised drinking water guidelines to prevent waterborne diseases' [online] www.who.int/water [Accessed 5 August 2011]

Yamamoto, H. (2003) 'New Public Management – Japan's practice' [online] www.iips. org/bp293e.pdf [Accessed 24 March 2011]

Yetano, A., Royo, S., and Acerete, B. (2009) 'What is driving the increasing presence of citizen participation initiatives?' [online] www.dteconz.unizar.es/dt2009-02.pdf [Accessed 23 June 2011]

Zipfel, T. and Gaventa, J. (2008) 'Policy perspectives: Citizen participation in local governance' [online] www.drc-citizenship.org/system/assets/1052724725/original/1052724725-zipfel_etal.2008-citizen.pdf/1299825763 [Accessed 20 July 2011]

ABOUT THE AUTHOR

Michael Anthony Tarallo is an international civil servant, whose career in international financial management spans 22 years. He has served in the United States, Austria, Kosovo, Israel, and Darfur, with special assignments in Jordan and Cyprus. He holds masters in political science and public administration and development. He is currently in charge of the financial resources for the United Nations peacekeeping mission in Darfur, currently the largest both in terms of funding and personnel.

He was born in New York and relocated to Rome, Italy, where he spent his childhood and teenage formative years. The international character of both his family- and professionally-driven relocations has allowed him to meet people from all walks of life and appreciate wide ranging cultures, customs, and traditions.

He has authored also P*ublic Administration: Key Issues Challenging Practitioners* (2012) and *UN Budgeting: A Sound Leap Forward* (2004).

He is married and a proud father of three children.